PAUL SIMON

··· *Transcribed* ···

PAUL SIMON ··· *Transcribed* ···

Transcriptions And Instruction By Mark Hanson

Published by:

ACCENT ON MUSIC
19363 Willamette Dr. #252
West Linn, OR 97068 USA

Copyright © 1993 by Mark D. Hanson
All tunes copyright © Paul Simon.
All Rights Reserved. Used By Permission.
First Printing 1993 10 9 8 7 6 5 4 3 2
Printed in the United States of America

Library of Congress Catalogue in Publication Data
Hanson, Mark D. 1951-
Paul Simon Transcribed.
1. Guitar—Methods—Self-Instruction. I. Title.

ISBN 0-936799-09-9 Paperback.

Table Of Contents

4
Introduction/The Artist/Simon's Technique
5
"Bookends" Instruction
6
"Bookends"
10
"American Tune" Instruction
11
"American Tune"
18
"Scarborough Fair" Instruction
19
"Scarborough Fair"
29
"The Late Great Johnny Ace" Instruction
30
"The Late Great Johnny Ace"
36
"Kathy's Song" Instruction
37
"Kathy's Song"
50
"The 59th Street Bridge Song (Feelin' Groovy)" Instruction
51
"The 59th Street Bridge Song (Feelin' Groovy)"
57
"Peace Like A River" Instruction
58
"Peace Like A River"
65
"Overs" Instruction
66
"Overs"
71
"For Emily, Whenever I May Find Her" Instruction
72
"For Emily, Whenever I May Find Her"
80
"Hearts And Bones" Instruction
81
"Hearts And Bones"
92
Tablature Guide
94
Other Books By Mark Hanson
96
Paul Simon Discography/Acknowledgments/The Author

Introduction

Welcome to *Paul Simon Transcribed*. In this book, we at Accent On Music have worked hard to give you the finest transcriptions possible for ten of Simon's best-loved tunes. The transcriptions are note-for-note from Simon's actual recordings. What is written here is what you hear on Simon's albums.

We have designed this book to accommodate all levels of guitarists, from relatively unskilled fingerpickers to professional players wishing to expand their repertoire. The songs are annotated as thoroughly as possible, so that you, the guitarist, will gain a full understanding of the guitar style of one of the greatest singer/songwriters of our time. The songs we have chosen are among Simon's best, and feature some of his most distinctive guitar work.

The Tablature

We have presented each song in both standard notation and tablature, so that you can choose whichever system serves you better. The tablature that we have developed we feel is the best and most accessible available. Not only do the numbers on the lines indicate your left-hand position on the fretboard, but the bold-print numbers indicate notes that are to be plucked by the thumb. With Simon's predilection for the Travis Pick (alternating-bass) style, this feature is very handy. Also, the rhythm markings under each tablature staff indicate the timing of each measure. For a full explanation of tablature, see the Tablature Guide in the back of this book.

The Artist

Paul Simon, of course, needs little introduction. He has been a world-renowned artist since the mid-'60s, when--as part of Simon and Garfunkel--he broke into the pop music scene with the stunning hit "Sounds Of Silence." A string of hits and highly refined albums followed, culminating with the Grammy Award-winning "Bridge Over Troubled Water" in 1970.

His solo career began in earnest in the early '70s, with hits like "Mother And Child Reunion," "Kodachrome" and "50 Ways To Leave Your Lover." It continues today with Simon searching out and recording increasingly sophisticated music with some of the greatest musicians from around the world.

Simon's Guitar Technique

Paul Simon is a highly skilled acoustic guitarist. He is not flashy, although you might argue with that statement after working through the instrumental sections of "Peace Like A River." He is a superb accompanist, whose strengths are superb tone, and an ability to compose distinctive guitar parts, ones that are immediately recognizable to the listener.

Simon's technique covers a variety of styles, from the thumb-and-one-finger Travis Picking style of Merle Travis and Doc Watson ("The Boxer"), to Brazilian bossa nova ("So Long, Frank Lloyd Wright"). His right-hand position is largely classical, with his palm arched fairly high above the strings. He picks with his flesh and fingernails, but at times wears a thumbpick. On occasion he rests several fingertips on the guitar top as he picks with his thumb, or thumb and index.

His left hand position is also classical, although he often will finger an *F* chord with his left thumb fretting the sixth string. I highly recommend watching his two *Concert In Central Park* videos. Close-up camera shots provide an excellent view of his hand position.

The alternating bass of the Travis Pick style is often apparent in Simon's playing. The most famous example, perhaps, is the "Boxer," but he uses it with artful variations throughout his repertoire. Even the signature opening guitar lick to "Hearts And Bones" is a variation of the alternating-bass style.

It is beyond the scope of this book to provide you with a thorough understanding of the Travis Picking style. However, if you need help understanding it, study my two books on the style: *The Art Of Contemporary Travis Picking*, and *The Art Of Solo Fingerpicking*. They will provide you with all of the technical essentials and understanding you will need to play these Paul Simon tunes. They are available in most retail music stores.

For intermediate players, some of these Paul Simon songs will be relatively easy to play, and others will be a challenge. The easiest tunes are "Bookends," "Scarborough Fair" and "The 59th Street Bridge Song (Feelin' Groovy)." But there is no doubt that all of these songs are worthy of the effort expended to play them.

Bookends

The Song

"Bookends" is the opening and closing theme to Side 1 of the original Simon and Garfunkel *Bookends* LP, released in 1968. With the advent of CDs, of course, the idea of a Side 1 and Side 2 on an album has become a quaint curiosity.

Simon uses "Bookends" as an instrumental theme to open the record. He places his capo at the 7th fret, playing from measures 1-23 as presented here. His final chord of the introduction, a C fingering (a G sound, with the capo), leads directly to the opening chord of the following tune, "Save The Life Of My Child."

When he and Garfunkel sing "Bookends," Simon places his capo at the 4th fret, to accommodate their voices. We have presented the notation for the entire song here, complete with both vocal parts.

The Technique

Simon begins with a *Dminor* chord, but his fingering is unlike the one most guitarists first learn. He places the *little* finger of the left hand on the second string, 3rd fret, and frets the fourth string at the 3rd fret with his ring finger. These two fingers remain in place--don't lift them!--for the duration of each *Dm/F* chord in the song. The index and middle fingers play their normal notes for a *Dminor* chord on the first and third strings, respectively. There is one alteration, however: the index finger and middle fingers lift off the strings so that you can pick the open first and third strings in the pattern (measure 2, for example).

To reproduce Simon's smooth sound, you must leave the index and middle fingers in place on the *Dm/F* until you are about to pick those strings again as open strings in the next measure. If you let go of the strings immediately after you pick them, the sustain and smoothness will be lost. Simply lift the index and middle fingers away from the strings as you pick them as open strings in the next measure.

Measures 5-7 use a simple C chord. In measure 8 you move onto an *F6* chord. Think of this as a simple three-finger *F*, with the little finger added on the second string, 3rd fret. After the initial pinch in measure 8, take your little finger off, leaving you with the three-finger *F*. Then move your ring finger from the fourth string to the fifth for the final pinch of measure 8.

At measure 9 you have a choice. You can either move your ring finger back to the fourth string for the first note, or you can sustain the fifth string with your ring finger and fret the fourth string with your little finger. However you choose to play it, by the third note of measure 9 your ring finger must be back on the third string so that the little finger can play the subsequent 3rd-fret note on the second string.

The remainder of the piece is simple repetition of measures 1-12, except for measures 24 and 51. In measure 24, Simon fingers a *C/G* chord, with the ring finger fretting the sixth string and little finger fretting the fifth.

In measure 51, Simon hammers on and pulls off with the index and middle fingers on the first and third strings, respectively. If you have trouble with hammer-ons and pull-offs, make sure that you lift your fingers far enough above the strings to gain some momentum before hitting the strings--an inch, perhaps. When you pull off, make sure you actually pluck the strings with the left-hand fingers. Don't just pull away from the strings, but pull them toward the floor before you release them. I often "push" off in this kind of circumstance. That means that I stretch the strings slightly toward the ceiling before I release them. Give that a try.

This hammer-on/pull-off combination is a characteristic move of Simon's. You can hear a similar technique in "I Am A Rock" on the *Sounds Of Silence.*

"Bookends"

Transcribed from *Bookends*

By Paul Simon

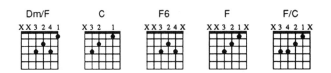

"Bookends"

7

"Bookends"

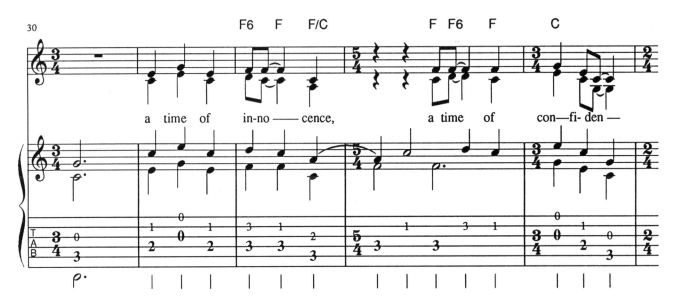

a time of in-no——cence, a time of con——fi- den —

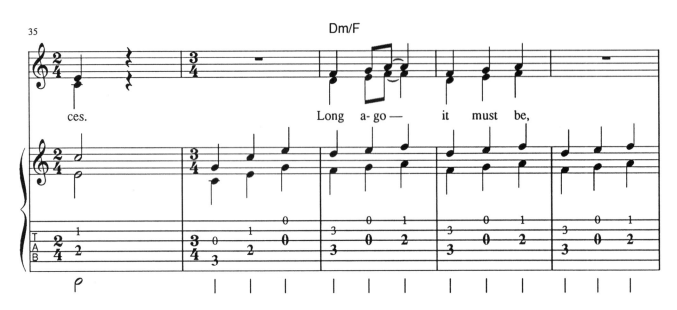

ces. Long a- go — it must be,

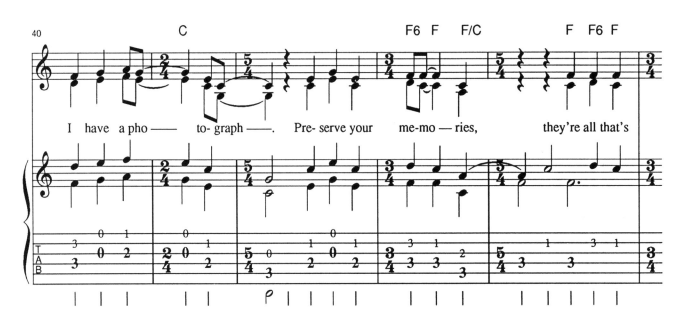

I have a pho——to- graph ——. Pre- serve your me-mo——ries, they're all that's

"Bookends"

left you.

9

American Tune

The Tune

Paul Simon has released performances "American Tune" on four albums: *There Goes Rhymin' Simon, Live Rhymin', Paul Simon--Greatest Hits, Etc.,* and *Simon and Garfunkel--Concert In Central Park*. This transcription is from *Paul Simon--Greatest Hits, Etc.*

Simon first recorded "American Tune" in the key of *C*, without a capo. Later he recorded it with his capo on the 2nd fret and sang in the key of *D*, although his guitar part maintained the key-of-C chord fingerings.

The opening lines of the melody of "American Tune" echo the hymn "O Sacred Head, Now Wounded" by 16th-century German composer Hans Leo Hassler.

The Technique

Simon uses several different picking patterns in "American Tune," picking extensively with his thumb and three fingers. In the opening phrase, for instance, Paul uses a technique common to the bossa nova guitar style: the fingers pick simultaneously, opposite the thumb. In measure 5, he pinches with the thumb and three fingers simultaneously. Even if you are not comfortable picking with your ring finger, give it a try. It will be difficult to imitate his style without it.

In measure 6, Simon starts an alternating-bass pattern with pinches on beats one and three. You'll find this same type of pattern in measures 13-14, 16-17 and 33-34, as well as later on in the tune. A fuller Travis Pick pattern with eighth notes picked by the fingers appears in the bridge section in measures 57-58 and 70.

Another pattern that he uses could be called a double-thumb arpeggio. Measures 7 and 11 are good examples. Here the first two beats start out like the alternating bass, but on the final two beats of the measure he completes an ascending arpeggio with notes picked by the fingers. Measures 21-24 also provide good examples of this arpeggio.

In measure 8 Paul moves from a standard *E* chord fingering to a first-inversion *E*: an *E/G#*. Finger the *E/G#* with your middle finger on the sixth (bass) string and your ring finger on the third string. You see this chord progression again in measure 79, this time with an alternate bass note on the second and fourth beats.

The *A minor* fingering in measure 9 is in the logical position following an *E/G#*. From the *E/G#*, slide your middle and ring fingers up one fret on their respective strings. Add your little finger on the 5th fret of the second string, or play both high-*E* notes as open first-string notes. Think of the *E7* in measure 10 as a normal *D7* fingering two frets higher.

A characteristic Paul Simon passage occurs in measure 15. He moves in parallel tenths from a *G* up to a *C*. (Parallel tenths are notes ten steps apart in a scale, moving the same direction.) You only need to finger one note for the *G* and *A minor* chords, as long as you pick the correct strings!

Finger the *G/B* (a *G* chord with a *B* as the lowest bass note) in measure 15 with your middle finger on the fifth string and little finger on the second. This is very important. Don't succumb to the temptation of fretting the fifth string with your index finger on the *G/B*. It will be a much smoother sounding progression if you can keep your index finger near the second string throughout measure 15. Sustain the *G/B* as you add your index finger on the first string for the *G7/B*. You'll find that this is nearly the same chord progression as "Feelin' Groovy," but ascending rather than descending.

The *G#dim7* in measure 16 should be fingered like an *E7* chord with the little finger added on the second string, 3rd fret. Your ring finger then must fret the 3rd fret of the fourth string. If stretching the ring finger to the 3rd fret is difficult, you may leave the fourth string open. A *D* note is a member of a *G#dim7* chord.

If you don't know the *C9* chord in measure 20, think of it this way: Play a normal *B7* chord at the end of the neck. Slide it up one fret toward the body of the guitar. Then move your little finger to the 3rd fret of the second string. *Voila,* a *C9*. The *Dm7* in measure 37 is fingered exactly like a first-position *D* chord, moved to the 5th fret.

A final note: Measures 9 and 23 are transcribed from verse 2 of the tune, as they were a bit more representative of what Paul normally plays. Also in verse 2, measure 8 is played like measure 79.

"American Tune"

Transcribed from *Paul Simon's Greatest Hits, etc.*

By Paul Simon

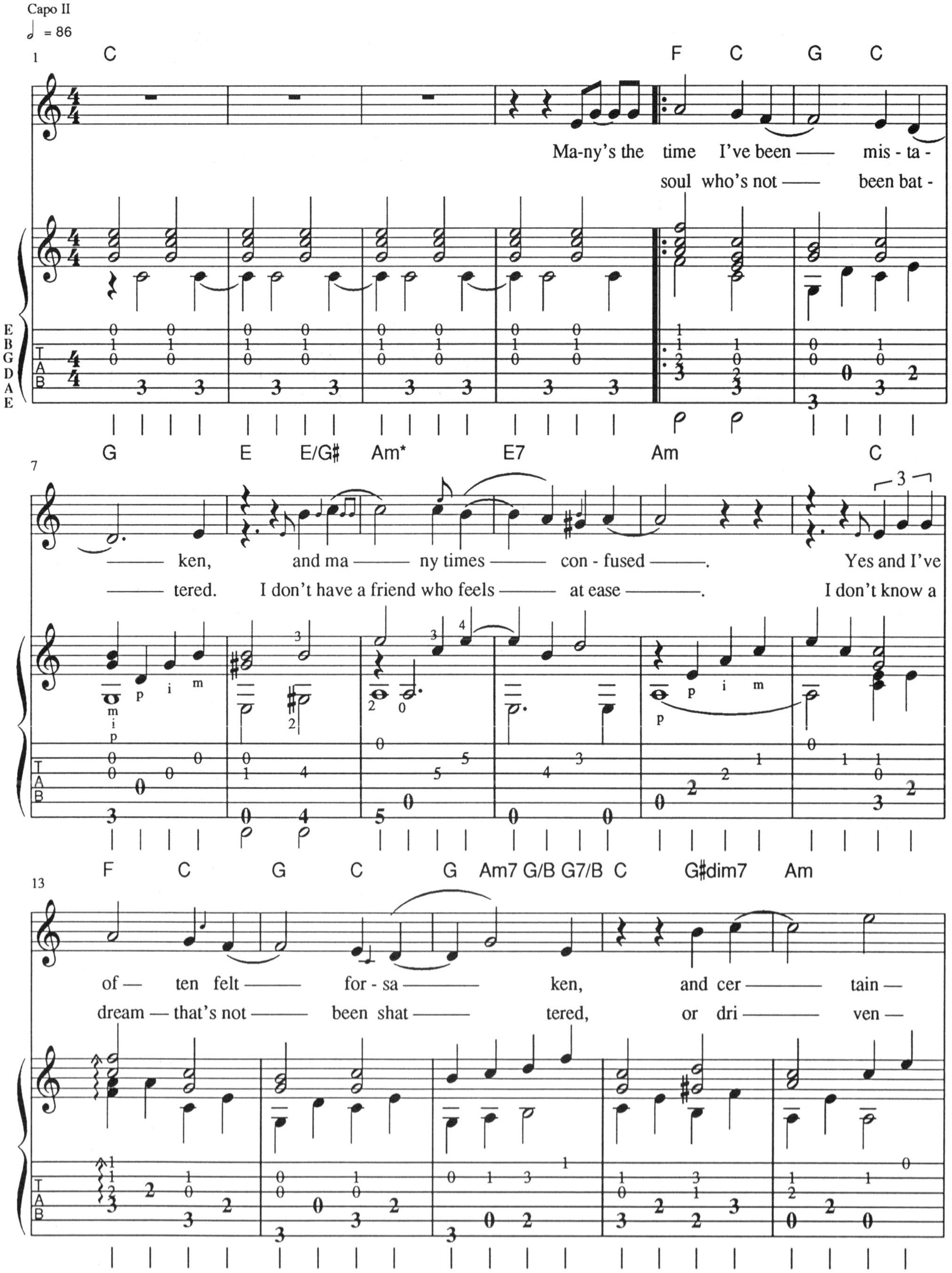

Capo II
𝅗𝅥 = 86
C F C G C
Ma-ny's the time I've been mis - ta -
soul who's not been bat -
G E E/G♯ Am* E7 Am C
ken, and ma ny times con - fused. Yes and I've
tered. I don't have a friend who feels at ease. I don't know a
F C G C G Am7 G/B G7/B C G♯dim7 Am
of - ten felt for - sa ken, and cer tain
dream that's not been shat tered, or dri ven
E B G D A E
p i m

"American Tune" Words & Music by Paul Simon. Copyright © 1973 PAUL SIMON. International copyright secured. All rights reserved. Used by permission.

C F G E E/G♯ Am* E7 Am Am7 G/B G7/B G♯dim7
IV
V

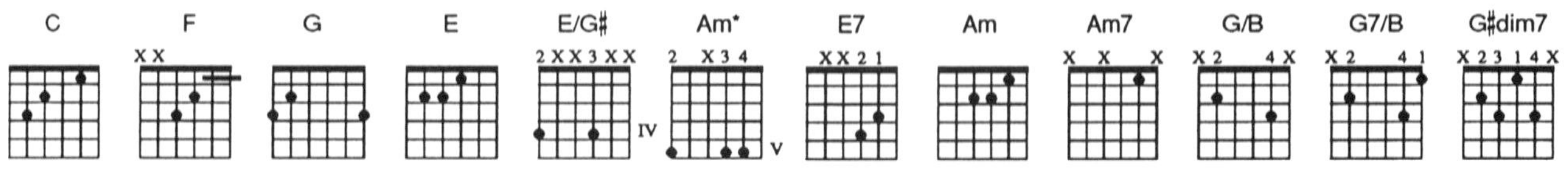

"American Tune"

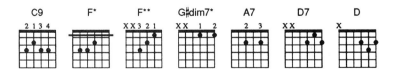

"American Tune"

"American Tune"

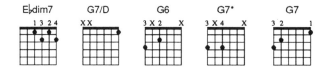

14

"American Tune"

15

"American Tune"

"American Tune"

Scarborough Fair

The Tune

"Scarborough Fair" is a traditional British folk song that Paul Simon and Art Garfunkel arranged for their *Parsley, Sage, Rosemary and Thyme* album. The recording was a major hit, and played a significant role in the soundtrack of the Dustin Hoffman/Anne Bancroft movie "The Graduate."

Simon and Garfunkel composed the "Canticle" vocal part to overlap the original melody of "Scarborough Fair." This produced a stunning montage of crossing voices backed by high-pitched guitar and harpsichord. In concert, however, Simon and Garfunkel performed "Scarborough Fair" without the "Canticle." This is how it is transcribed here, with both vocal parts notated. The vocals were transcribed from *Simon and Garfunkel--The Concert In Central Park*. The guitar transcription is from *Parsley, Sage Rosemary and Thyme*, since that version contains the recognizable introduction.

The vocal arranging is first class, as you would expect. The upper vocal part here is the melody, sung by Garfunkel. The lower vocal part is Simon's harmony. This changes very artfully during measures 85-90. In measure 85, Garfunkel skies to a higher harmony while Simon shifts up to the melody. They shift back down to their normal parts in measure 86, only to shift up again in measures 87-90. This same interplay of voices occurs in measures 109-114.

The Technique

Paul Simon's "Scarborough Fair" guitar arrangement is inspired. Several factors make it interesting, as well as beautiful. First, Simon places his capo at the 7th fret. This accommodates Garfunkel's vocal range, but it also produces a crystalline treble tone not normally associated with a mid-rangy steel-string guitar. You might want to capo it lower, if you don't sing as high as Garfunkel! Second, Simon juxtaposes 6/8 and 3/4 meters throughout his arrangement. A quick explanation of the difference: 6/8 and 3/4 meters each contain six eighth notes in a measure. In 6/8 time, the emphasized notes are the first and fourth. In 3/4 time, the emphasized notes are the first, third and fifth. The speed of the eight notes is the same for both meters. The vocal meter in "Scarborough Fair" is 3/4 throughout the tune, so there are times when two meters are happening simultaneously.

Simon's main riff is notated in measures 4-5. (Measures 1-3 are an introduction. We'll come back to those in a moment.) To produce the Am* chord in measure 4, finger a normal C chord. Next, lift your ring finger off the fifth string and slide the index and middle fingers up two frets to Am*. The Aadd9 chord in measure 5 is a normal first-position Am chord with the index finger lifted off the second string. When you change between these two chords, slide your middle finger lightly on the fourth string.

The right-hand picking pattern for this riff is: *p-a-i-p-m-i* (thumb-ring-index-thumb-middle-index). To learn this pattern, break it into two parts: thumb-ring-index, then thumb-middle-index. Your three fingers pick the three treble strings, while the thumb alternates between the fifth and fourth strings. If you don't use your ring finger, use your middle finger twice in the pattern. I have had success teaching the pattern in this way: Think of the third string as the center of a five-string pattern. (You won't use the sixth string in this pattern.) First you play the *outside* strings (fifth and first) followed by the center string (third). Then you play the *inside* strings (fourth and second) followed again by the center string (third). If that helps you to remember it, great! Practice this main riff until it is comfortable.

Now, back to the introduction. Measure one is the main riff. Measure two is the same picking pattern, but with the left-hand ring finger added on the fifth string, as if you were playing a C fingering at the 3rd, 4th and 5th frets. For measure 3, slide this C fingering to the end of the neck, and lift your index finger. That gives you the Cmajor7 chord.

The next new chord is in measure 9. Finger the bass note of the G chord with your ring finger and hold on for the entire measure. The C/G is produced by adding your index and middle fingers to their normal locations for a C chord *as you sustain the low G note*. In measure 10, you are right back to your main riff. In measure 13, finger a normal C chord and pick your main *p-a-i-p-m-i* pattern. The same pattern occurs in measure 14, on an Am7 chord.

Measure 15 is in 3/4 time. The emphasized notes are the pinches on the first, third and fifth notes of the measure. Pinch with your thumb and ring or middle, followed by your index finger picking the open third string. In measure 16 you are back to your main riff. Measure 20 contains a walk-up in the bass to a C chord in measure 21, where you again play your main picking pattern. Measure 22 is the same chord progression as "Feelin' Groovy." Here again you are in 3/4 time, with the pinches on the first, third and fifth notes of the measure. The index again picks the open third string between pinches. Make sure you use your middle and little fingers to fret the G/B chord.

Fret the G chord in measure 23 with your ring finger on the sixth string. Sustain it as you pull off from the C/G chord later in the measure. In measure 27, Simon uses his characteristic double hammer-on/pull-off on the C/G to lead into the main riff once again and verse 2.

At measure 128 Simon repeats the introductory passage, and ends with a 12th-fret harmonic on the first string. To produce that harmonic, make sure you lightly touch the first string *12 frets above the capo position*. Then pluck the string sharply to produce a ringing harmonic.

"Scarborough Fair/Canticle"

Transcribed from *Parsley, Sage Rosemary And Thyme*

Arranged By Paul Simon and Art Garfunkel

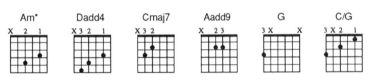

"Scarborough Fair/Canticle"

Pars — ley, sage —, rose — ma — ry and thyme —

Re — mem — ber me — to one who lives there —

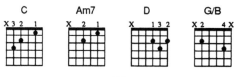

"Scarborough Fair/Canticle"

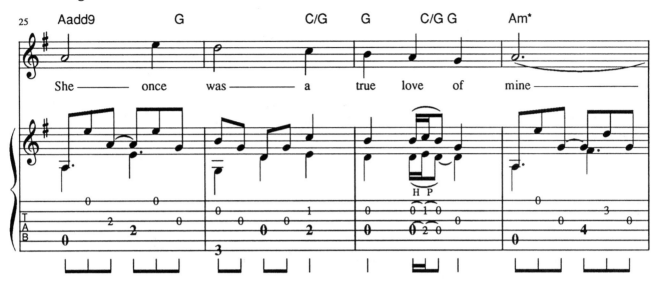

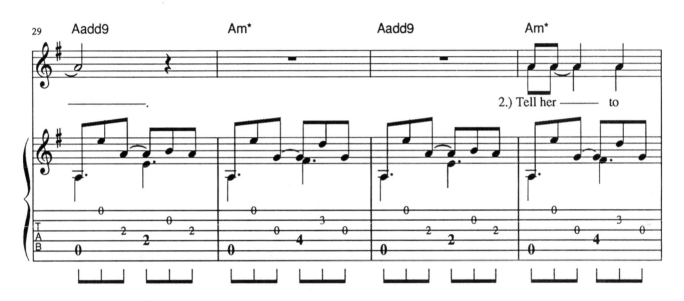

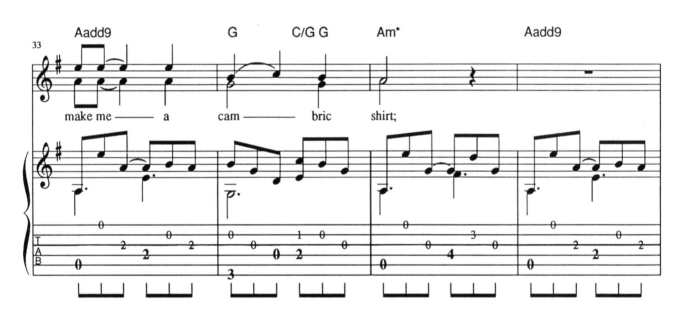

"Scarborough Fair/Canticle"

"Scarborough Fair/Canticle"

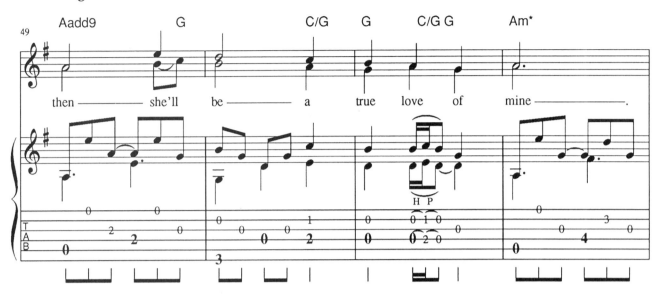

then ——— she'll be ——— a true love of mine ——— .

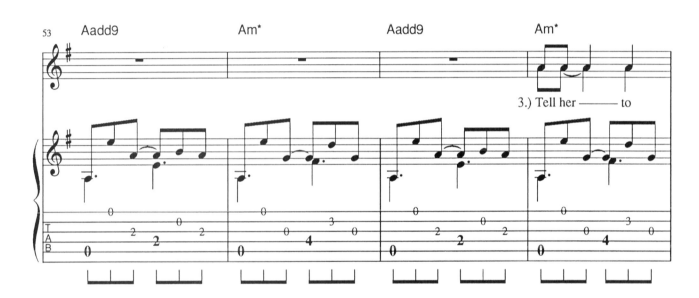

3.) Tell her ——— to

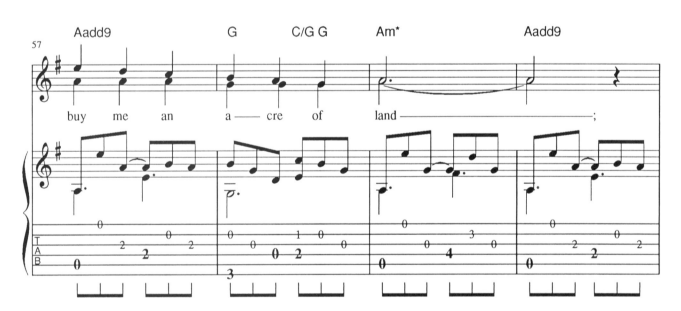

buy me an a — cre of land ——————— ;

"Scarborough Fair/Canticle"

"Scarborough Fair/Canticle"

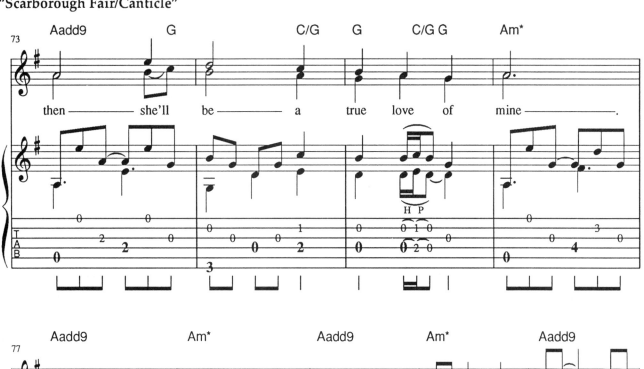

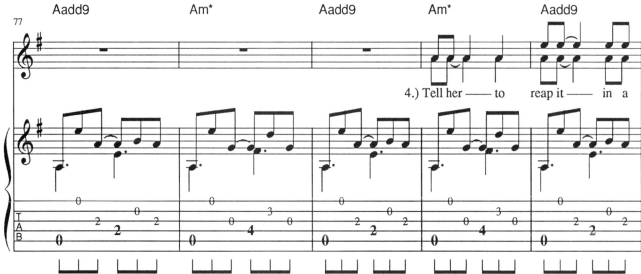

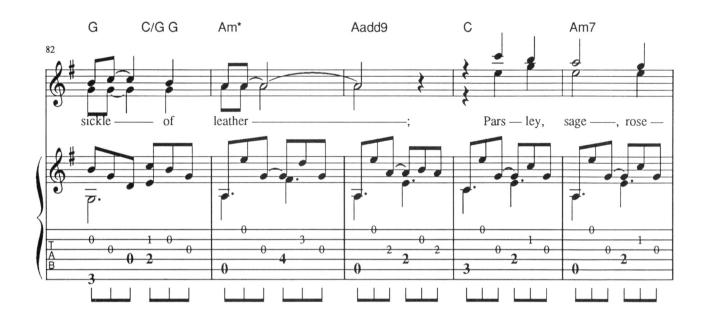

"Scarborough Fair/Canticle"

"Scarborough Fair/Canticle"

"Scarborough Fair/Canticle"

The Late Great Johnny Ace

The Tune

The first-ever performance of "The Late Great Johnny Ace" was released as part of the *Simon And Garfunkel--Concert In Central Park* video. This transcription is taken from that video. One rather frightening aspect of the performance occurred when an audience member ran toward Simon onstage as he sang the final verse about the death of John Lennon.

Simon tunes his guitar down one whole-step in "The Late Great Johnny Ace." I have chosen to write the standard notation in the key of the fingering, rather than down one whole-step as it actually sounds. If you want to play this tune at the written pitch, don't tune your strings down. But to play along with Simon's recording, you must retune your strings.

One very interesting aspect of "The Late Great Johnny Ace" is Simon's increasingly sophisticated harmonic sense. This tune is in the key of D, but he starts out with two chords that aren't even in the key of D: *Bbmaj7* (the chord built on the flatted sixth note of a D scale) and E. He doesn't play a D chord until measure 17.

In measures 18-29 he uses a number of advanced harmonic techniques that blend beautifully with the melody. In measure 17 he is in the key of D, but in measure 18 he immediately modulates (changes key) to G by using a D7 chord. Next he's heading for the key of *Eminor* in measure 22. To get there he uses a flatted sixth chord again, this time the flatted sixth of the key of *Eminor*: the C in measure 20.

Another technique he uses in this passage is a common-tone modulation. He moves smoothly from the C9 to a B7(#9) chord in measure 21 by maintaining the highest pitch note between the two. You'll notice that this common note, a D, is also the vocal melody note in measure 21.

Once Simon arrives on the *Eminor* chord in measure 22, he uses it to move on to the key of *Bminor* (measure 24). Another common-tone movement occurs between the *Bm7* and the *Gmaj7* in measure 25: the highest-pitch note of the two chords is the same, again a D. The entire phrase from measure 24-28 can also be interpreted as being in the key of D. (All of these chords belong in the key of D.) But when you expect to hear the D chord in measure 29 after the A7, he gives you a "deceptive cadence," and goes off to his original flatted sixth chord again, the *Bbmaj7*.

In measure 54, Simon again arrives at a C9 chord, but instead of playing the B7(#9) that we expect to hear after hearing it in measures 20-21, he goes to the key of F. In measure 59 he uses the *Bbmaj7* chord (which is in the key of F) as a bridge back to the beginning and the key of D. This is sophisticated composing, to say the least.

The Technique

Closely study the chord diagrams for this piece before you spend too much time on it. Simon's chording seldom involves fingering extraneous notes. For instance, the *Bbmaj 7* is fingered with three fingers, leaving the first string open for the E note. The E chord that follows is a one-finger chord--the index finger frets the third string at the 1st fret. Hammer-on the 2nd-fret note (A) with your middle finger. Pick with the thumb and three fingers of the right hand.

The chords in measures 15-17 are normal first-position fingerings. In measure 18, Simon plays a D7 chord, but fingers it like a C7 moved to the 3rd, 4th and 5th frets. In measure 20, the C9 is fingered like a normal B7 with two alterations: move one fret higher (toward the body of the guitar), and move your little finger to the second string, 3rd fret. To finger the B7(#9) in the next measure, maintain the position of your little finger from the C9, but move the other three fingers one fret lower.

The F#7(#5) in measure 23 is fingered with a barre at the 2nd fret. The middle finger frets the third string at the 3rd fret, and the ring finger frets the second string at the 3rd fret. The ring finger will lift off the string, then finger its note again during the measure. A similar on-off-on motion occurs in measure 24, this time with the middle finger. To change from the *Gmaj7* in measure 25 to the subsequent *Bminor*, move your index finger from the sixth string to a 2nd-fret barre. Maintain the other three fingers. In measures 28 and 31, Simon lets go of his A chord, and frets only the C#, second string 2nd fret, to ensure a clean pull-off.

In measure 32, Simon begins a bluesy parallel-sixth figure in the key of D. This is a common fingerstyle blues pattern, with the fingers picking *on the bea*t and the thumb picking *off* the beat. Make sure you pick this in a triplet rhythm: The finger notes last twice as long as the thumb notes. Count 1-2-3 evenly as you play. The finger notes occur on 1 and the thumb notes occur on three. This passage is arpeggiated in triplets on the *Hearts And Bones* album. If you want to imitate that pattern, pick *p-i-a* for each beat (thumb-index-ring; **0**-4-3, **0**-5-5, **0**-4-3, **0**-0-0, etc., in the tablature).

Simon barres at the 3rd fret in measure 43-44 for both the *Abdim7* and *Gm7* chords. To finger the A7(b9) chord in measure 45, think of it as a normal D fingering, moved one fret higher and one string over. Then add your little finger on the first string, 3rd fret, to complete the chord. In measure 53, Simon goes back to his straight-eighth-note rhythm, moving into his 3/4 meter section in the key of F.

This leads back to measure 3 at the beginning. From there, play until measure 27, singing verse 5. Then play the Coda.

The Coda on the *Hearts And Bones* studio recording was composed by Phillip Glass. The Coda transcribed here is Simon's guitar part ending the live performance on the *Concert In Central Park* video.

"The Late Great Johnny Ace"

Transcribed from *Simon & Garfunkel--Concert In Central Park*

By Paul Simon

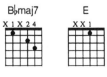

"Late Great Johnny Ace"

"Late Great Johnny Ace"

"Late Great Johnny Ace"

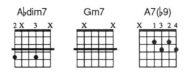

"Late Great Johnny Ace"

Kathy's Song

The Tune

"Kathy's Song" was recorded as a Paul Simon solo on the *Sounds Of Silence* album. With its simple yet beautiful melody, sparkling guitar work and poetic lyrics, it is little wonder "Kathy's Song" was included on *Simon And Garfunkel's Greatest Hits* album.

Because of the slight variations of the melody from one verse to the next, we have notated the entire song from beginning to end, even though it required 13 pages to print. But don't be alarmed. There aren't 13 pages of guitar licks to learn. Much of the guitar work is repeated from verse to verse. The structure of this piece is: two verses, instrumental, two verses, instrumental, two verses, final instrumental.

The Technique

"Kathy's Song" perhaps is the best recorded example of Simon's Travis Picking ability. This song, and others like it from Simon's early years, taught me much about using the treble strings sparingly and tastefully.

Measures 1-4 start with a one-finger chord, with the bass alternating between an *F#* on the fourth string and a *G* on the third. In measure 5, Simon arrives at his main riff for the tune, the *G-C/G-G* chord progression. As in "Scarborough Fair," you must finger your *G* chord with your ring finger on the sixth string, 3rd fret. This keeps your index and middle fingers available for their notes on the *C/G* chord. Also, make sure you sustain that bass note as you finger the rest of the *C/G* chord. Otherwise, it will not sound as full and flowing as Simon's version.

In measure 5, pick with the thumb alone on the first beat. On beat 2, pinch the second and fourth strings with your middle and thumb, respectively, and immediately hammer-on with your index and middle fingers of the left hand (as you sustain the bass note with your left-hand ring finger!). If that hammer-on is difficult for you, practice just the pinch and the hammer-on (beat two). Lift your index and middle fingers a good inch above the strings before the hammer-on so that you have good momentum into the strings. Also, make sure you hold the strings down after the hammer-on.

On the last two beats of measure 5, play a thumb-middle-thumb pattern on the *C/G*, followed by a pull-off on the final eighth note. To pull-off, either pull the strings slightly toward the floor before releasing them, or push them toward the ceiling slightly before the release. If you simply pull your fingers away from the strings you will not produce strong-sounding notes. In measure 9, Simon starts verse 1. Through measure 14 he plays one "pinch" Travis Pick pattern on each chord, starting with a *G* and a *C/G*. In measures 10 and 11, make sure your right thumb is picking the sixth string, not the fifth, on the first and third beats. In measure 13, Simon finally picks the first string. This high *G* note is very effective at this point, since the listener hasn't heard it yet. This is an example of what I mean about Simon using the first string sparingly and tastefully.

In measure 14 he plays a simple *Aminor* chord with the "pinch" pattern. In measures 15-16 he speeds up his harmonic movement (the speed at which he changes chords), using two chords per measure. The *Am/G* is fingered just like the previous *Aminor*, except that you release your index finger from the second string, and fret the sixth string with your little finger. The little finger should reach to the bass string at a low enough angle that the fleshy part of the finger touches the fifth string as it frets the sixth. This mutes the open fifth string, which will make your *Am/G* chord a much cleaner sound. For the final 1-1/2 beats of measure 15, simply let go of all the strings with the left hand. Move to a *C* chord for measure 16. Halfway through measure 16 Simon moves to a one-finger *G/B* chord. Use your middle finger to fret the low *B* note.

In measure 17, Simon plays a barre *Bminor* chord at the 2nd fret. But he uses the sixth string as his lowest bass note, hence a *Bm/F#*. In measure 18 he again picks the first string, for the first time since the *G* in measure 13. The *G** chord in measure 19 is a barre *G* chord, which works nicely with the *Bm/F#* chords that surround it. In measure 21, Simon returns to his original *G* fingering, adding a walk-up in the bass to the *C* chord in measure 22. In measure 23 he again picks the first string. In measure 25 he plays the *Am/G* chord again, this time sustaining it throughout the measure. Notice that the final bass note of measure 25 is not the higher-pitched alternate bass note, but a repeat of the sixth string. In measure 26 he plays a *D* chord, leaving out his normal bass note on the third beat. Measure 27-30 are nearly identical to each other. Each adds the two *C/G* notes to the low *G* bass note on the third beat of the measure.

The other verses are the same, so let's take a look at the instrumentals between verses and at the end of the song. In measure 51, Simon adds his *C/G* to the low *G* note on the sixth string, then simply slides this fingering two frets up the neck, toward the body of the guitar. He also adds his little finger on the first string, 5th fret, in measure 53. The instrumental in measures 100-104 is identical except that he waits until the third of these four measures to play the high note on the first string.

The instrumental starting at measure 148 contains some interesting changes. Paul's alternating bass line disappears on the fourth beat of each measure: He picks the sixth string again, as he did in measure 25. He also is picking a melody, starting with the open third string. In measure 149 he hammers-on. Use your middle or index finger for this hammer-on, while you sustain the sixth-string note with your ring finger. By measure 152, Simon is right back into his accompaniment pattern, with slight changes.

Notice where Simon used the first string in this accompaniment. He used it only between lines of the vocal, where it could be clearly heard and would add interest where it was needed.

"Kathy's Song"

Transcribed from *Sounds Of Silence*

By Paul Simon

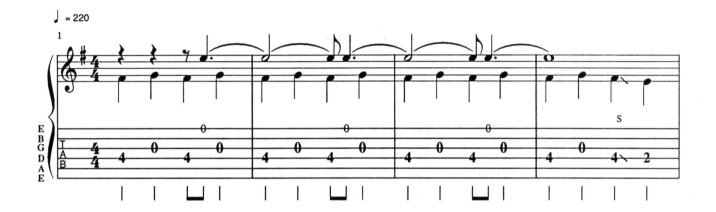

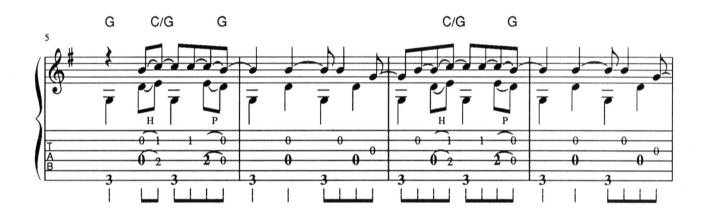

1.) I hear the driz —— zle of —— the rain ——.

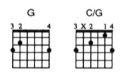

"Kathy's Song"

"Kathy's Song"

"Kathy's Song"

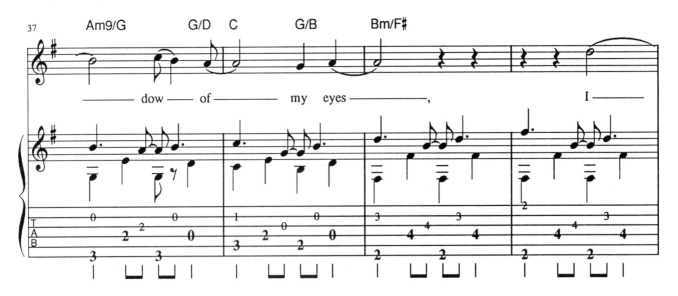

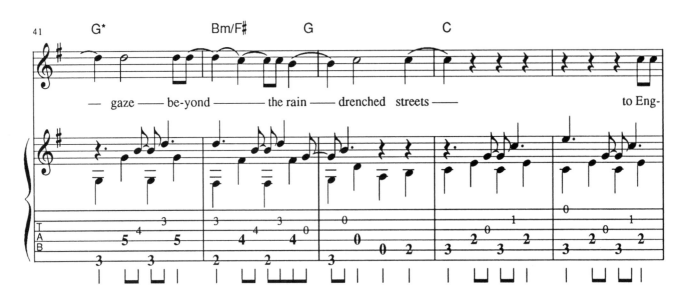

40

"Kathy's Song"

"Kathy's Song"

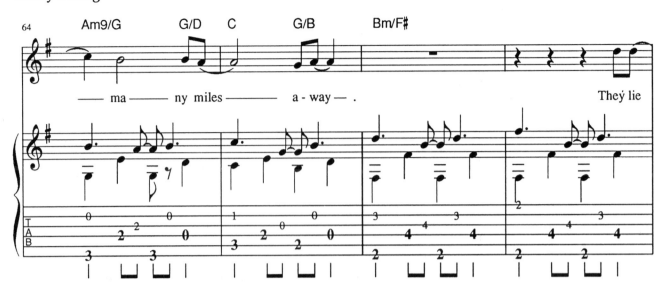

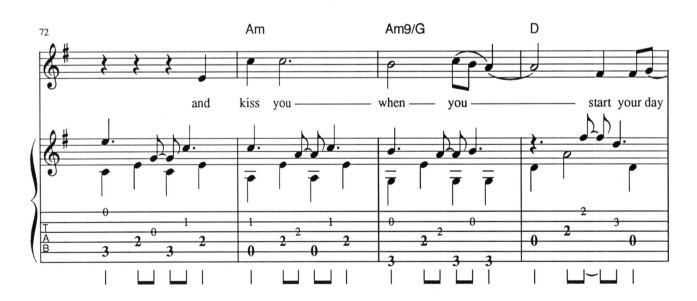

42

"Kathy's Song"

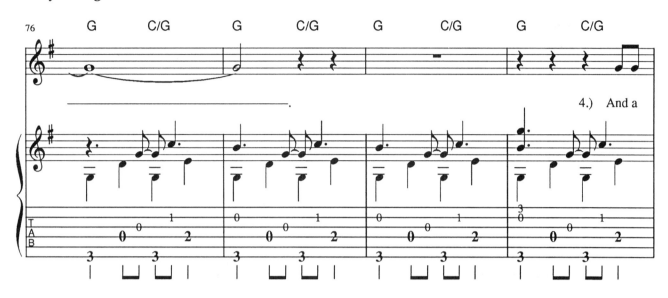

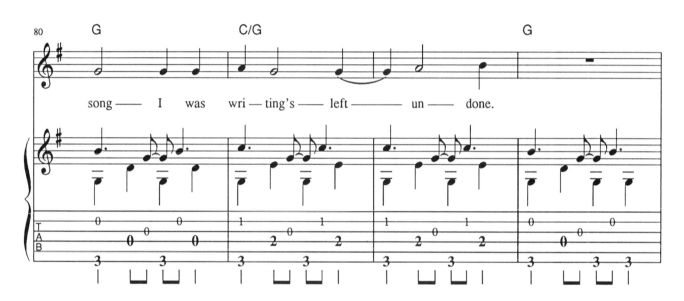

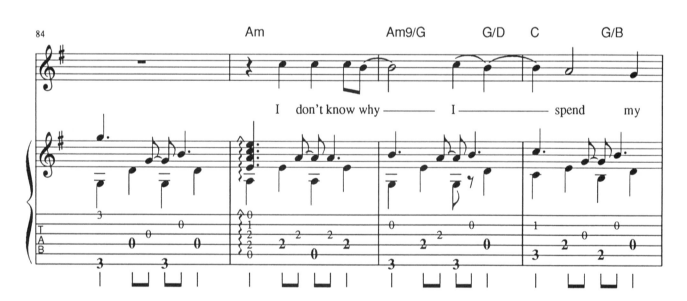

43

"Kathy's Song"

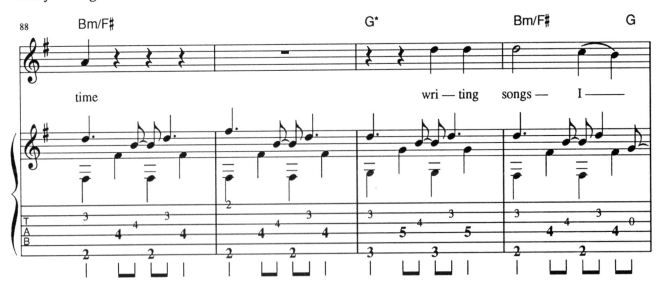

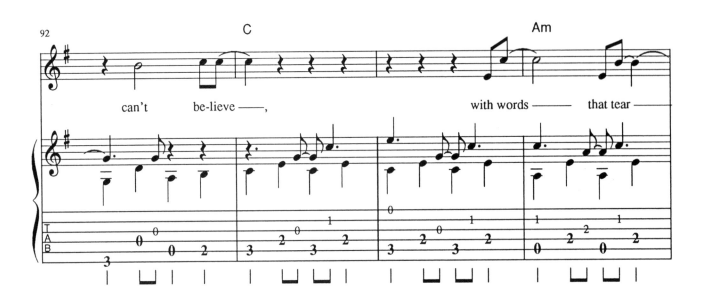

"Kathy's Song"

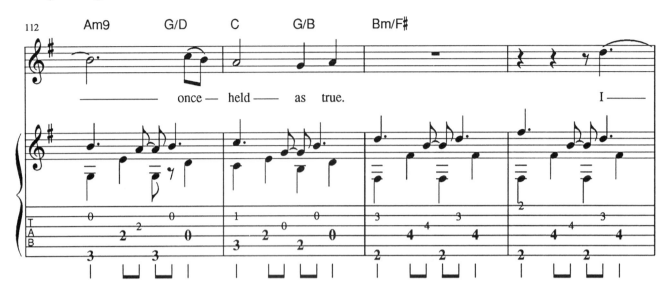

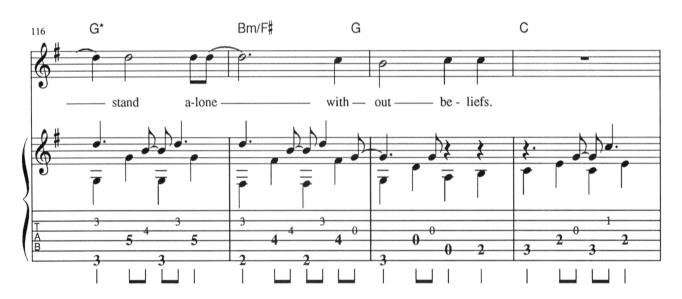

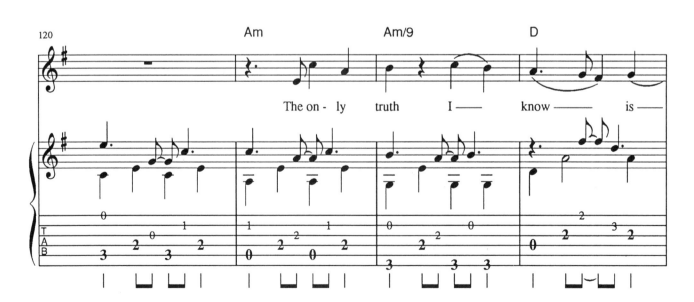

"Kathy's Song"

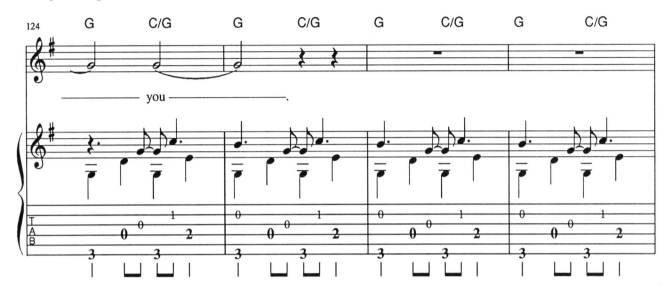

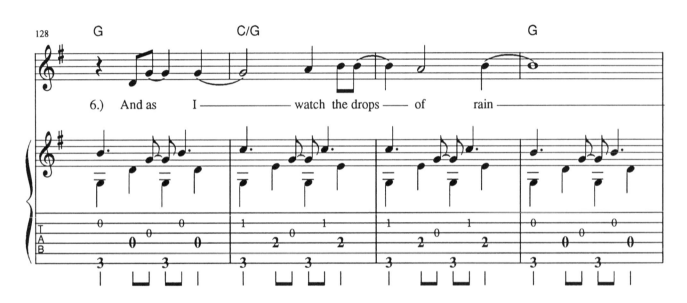

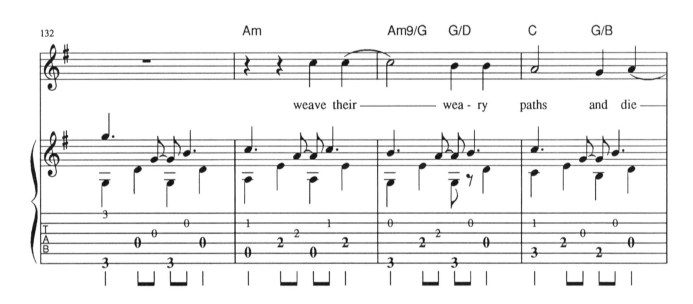

"Kathy's Song"

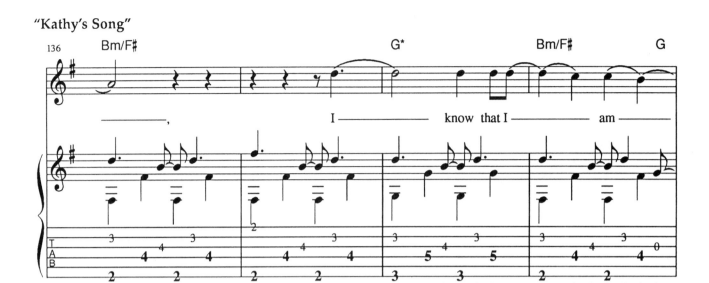

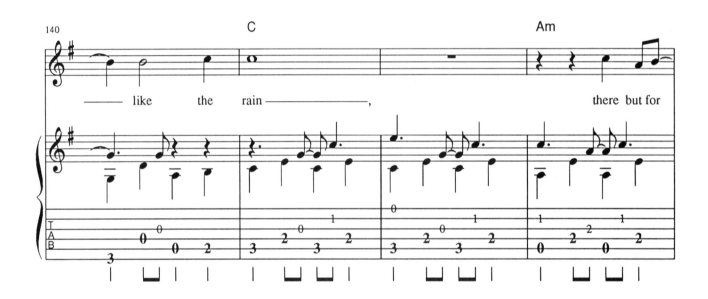

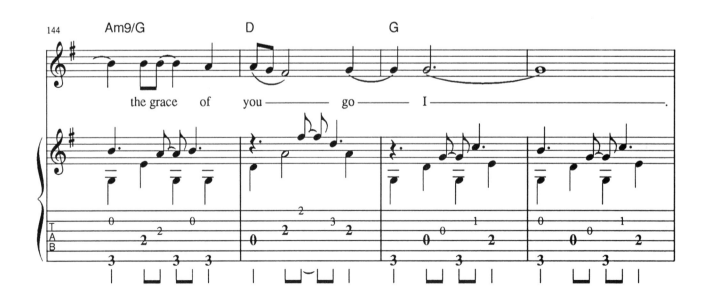

48

"Kathy's Song"

59th Street Bridge Song (Feelin' Groovy)

The Tune

This song took a catch word of the youth movement of the '60s--"groovy"-- and turned it into a hit song. It is very simple in its construction--the guitar part consists of a four-chord progression that repeats endlessly. Yet the song's sense of humor, combined with its sprightly rhythm and clever lyrics, keeps it from becoming dated.

This guitar rendition is transcribed from *Parsley, Sage, Rosemary and Thyme*. The vocals are from the *Simon And Garfunkel Concert In Central Park* video, where the two-part vocals were not obscured at all by the extra vocals added to the studio version.

The Technique

The four chords that Simon uses in "Feelin' Groovy" are *C*, *G/B*, *Am7*, and *G*. Except for the two-fingered *G/B*, and an occasional *C* chord that uses both fretted bass notes, all of these chords can be fingered with one finger! However, I suggest for *C* that you finger an entire *C* chord in case you pick some wrong strings. The *G/B* should be fingered with the little finger on the second string, 3rd fret, and the middle finger on the fifth string, 2nd fret.

Am7 requires that you only fret the second string, 1st fret. This chord has a *D* in it, so you could call it a *D7sus4/A*, but for ease we will call it an *Am7*. The *G* that follows the *Am7* requires your ring finger to fret the sixth string, 3rd fret.

The picking pattern for "Feelin' Groovy" is an adaptation of the Travis Pick. Measures 13-14 provide a good example of the normal flow of Simon's guitar part. The alternating bass is apparent on the *G/B* and *Am7* chords, but you have a drone bass (repeating the same note) under the *C* and *G* chords. Simon's fingers are busy picking out treble notes. The index finger is expecially busy picking the open third string between beats. Use either the middle finger (second string) or the ring finger (first string) for the treble notes in the on-the-beat pinches in this passage.

The ending in measures 54-55 is transcribed fom the *Concert In The Park* video, since the studio version uses a fade out at the end. Also, the final two measures on page 56 are Simon's introduction from that video. They can be substituted for measures 1 and 2.

One very interesting aspect of this piece is the tuning. In the live version, Simon uses standard tuning, but omits the characteristic instrumental section presented here in measures 8-10. That section must be played in Drop-*D* tuning (the bass string is tuned down one whole-step) to exactly match what is on the *Parsley, Sage, Rosemary and Thyme* album. The open sixth-string note in measure 9 is a *D* (ignoring the capo) on *Parsley, Sage, Rosemary and Thyme*. I have taken the liberty to write it as an *E* in this transcription, figuring that most people will play this tune in standard tuning, and *E* is the lowest note you can produce in standard tuning.

The bends in measure 10 are much easier in Drop-*D* tuning, since the string is looser and you bend the string two frets farther from the capo. If you want to play the opening in Drop-*D* tuning, substitute the first measure of the last system on page 56 for measure 10. If you play in Drop-*D*, all of the **3**s on the bass string must be played as **5**s throughout the tune. (See the asterisk * in measure 2.)

"The 59th Street Bridge Song (Feelin' Groovy)"

Transcribed from *Parsley, Sage Rosemary And Thyme*

By Paul Simon

1.) Slow down, you move too fast —.

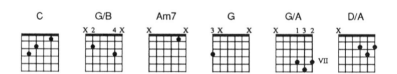

"The 59th Street Bridge Song (Feelin' Groovy)"

"The 59th Street Bridge Song (Feelin' Groovy)"

"The 59th Street Bridge Song (Feelin' Groovy)"

promises to keep. I'm dap- pled and drow- sy and rea- dy to sleep let the

morn- ing time drop all its pe- tals on me ————. Life —, I love you.

All — is — groovy ————. Ba — da — da ———.

55

"The 59th Street Bridge Song (Feelin' Groovy)"

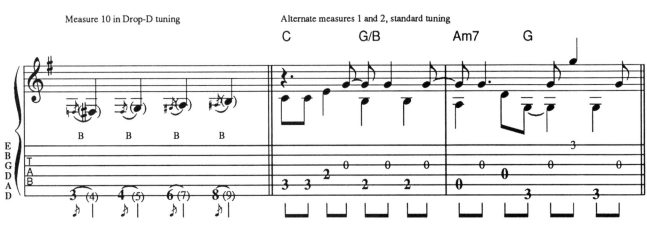

Measure 10 in Drop-D tuning

Alternate measures 1 and 2, standard tuning

Peace Like A River

The Tune

"Peace Like A River" is from Paul Simon's first solo album, released shortly after the breakup of Simon and Garfunkel. It was simply entitled *Paul Simon*.

Like "The Late Great Johnny Ace," this tune uses standard tuning tuned down one whole-step to *D G c f a d'*, lowest pitch to highest. Simon did this to accommodate his vocal range. To accommodate the student, the standard notation for "Peace Like A River" is written in the key of the chord fingerings, namely *E*, even though it sounds in the key of *D* because of the lowered tuning. People with absolute pitch may be bothered by this presentation, but for the vast majority of students using this book, it will work well.

If you want to have another instrumentalist read from the music with you, simply capo at the 2nd fret, or don't tune down at all. Then the pitch of the guitar will match the actual pitch written here in standard notation. But be aware, to play along with Simon's recording, you must tune the strings down one whole-step.

The Technique

"Peace Like A River" is a great example of Paul Simon's ability to play a searing lead guitar part.

The tune starts with a bluesy opening riff that repeats throughout the piece. This riff is a great example of Simon's ability to compose a guitar part that is distinctive and memorable. Notice that he is far away from the Travis Pick style for this riff, with the bass notes mostly off the beat. The Travis Pick starts in measure 7 with just the alternating-bass pattern, no fingers. He uses this simple alternating bass to good effect in "Homeward Bound" as well.

In measure 10 he starts a regular "outside-in" Travis Pick pattern (*p-m-p-i*). In measure 13 he strums on the second and fourth beats. Don't be confused by the directions of the arrows in the notation. Each strum is a down-up (toward the floor, then toward the ceiling). This Travis Pick/strum pattern continues until measure 18, where he plays his opening *Em7* riff again. Verse 2 is very similar to verse 1, but he introduces new chords in measures 32-33, an *Am/G* (little finger frets the sixth string) and a *D7/F#* (finger the sixth-string note with the middle finger or the thumb).

The bridge section begins in measure 35 with a walk-up from *G* to *G/B*, then back to *Am7*. This walk-up chord progression is nearly identical to "Feelin' Groovy," except Simon plays it in the ascending, rather than descending, direction. The rhythm in measures 37, 39, 41, 43 and 45 contains some syncopations. Accents off the beat are the rule here. In each measure, the second chord arrives an eighth note before the third beat. Count this as 1 & 2 &, with the second chord arriving on the & after 2.

You can play the notes in measure 49 by placing a barre over the three treble strings at the 7th fret, then hammering-on (and pulling-off) the second and third strings with the middle and ring fingers, respectively. The strums on the first beat of measures 50 and 51 are upswings--toward the bass string from the treble.

The lead-guitar section, measures 52-57, is picked with the fingers and thumb, although it may sound like a flat-picked lead guitar passage. Simon's trick is to use a combination of open and fretted strings to produce the unusual juxtaposition of notes in this section.

In measure 52 slide your middle finger on the third string to the 9th fret. Then add your index finger on the 8th fret of the first string. The right hand pattern in 52-53 is something of a drone Travis Pick: thumb-middle-thumb-index, with the thumb always picking the same string. In measure 54, bend the second string with the ring finger at the 7th fret *before* you pick it on the second beat. Pick it, then release the bend for the next note. Next, fret the second string, 5th fret, with your index finger.

Picking the two open strings next gives your left hand a moment to move to the third and fourth strings for the next chord in measure 54. Finger the *Em7** with your index and ring fingers. Move these same fingers to the fourth and fifth strings for the *Em9* in measures 55-56. In measure 57, the one tricky thing may be to pick the fifth string twice in a row, alternating the thumb and index of the right hand. In measure 58 you are right back to the opening *Em7* riff.

Simon recorded a second guitar part over the main part transcribed here. They are separated nicely in the stereo mix. The second part adds some extra notes to certain chords, in particular the *G* in measures 11-12, 26-27 and 66-67. In 66-67 I have taken the liberty to arrange the main guitar part to imitate the notes the second guitar part adds.

The guitar solo beginning in measure 80 is not quite identical to the first solo. It starts out the same way, but in measure 83 he plays a hammer-on figure missing from the original. This figure places the index- and middle-finger notes opposite where they were rhythmically in the first solo.

The ending involves bending the sixth string substantially in measures 90 and 92. Be aware that this is easier to do with the strings tuned down one whole-step than it is at standard tuning.

"Peace Like A River"

Transcribed from *Paul Simon*

By Paul Simon

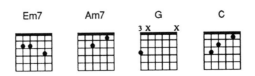

"Peace Like A River"

"Peace Like A River"

"Peace Like A River"

61

"Peace Like A River"

"Peace Like A River"

63

"Peace Like A River"

Oh ———, oh —, oh ————————, I'm gonna be up for a while ————

Overs

The Tune

"Overs" is another song from the Simon and Garfunkel era that features Paul Simon nearly entirely as a soloist. Garfunkel appears intermittently with a harmony part, and sings the bridge as the lead voice. The tune is featured on the *Bookends* album, from where this transcription was taken.

The Technique

The guitar accompaniment of "Overs" features a number of by-now familiar chord fingerings, progressions and techniques. For instance, in measure 7 we see nearly the identical *C-G/B-Am7* descending passage that "Feelin' Groovy" uses. Measure 9 uses the *D7/F#* that we saw in "Peace Like A River." And in measure 32, we see the same *Dminor* figure that starts "Bookends." He uses a healthy number of diminished seventh chords, with several different fingerings.

In "Overs," Simon also switches freely between a straight eighth-note rhythm and a triplet feel. The difference is this: In a straight-eighth rhythm, there are two eighth notes for each beat, and they are evenly spaced rhythmically (their duration is identical). In triplet or "swing" time, each beat is divided into three parts. Two eighth notes in triplet time occur on the first and third subdivisions of each beat, like this: **1** 2 **3** **1** 2 **3**. Listen closely to the recording to imitate Simon's rhythmic feel.

In measure 1, Simon starts with a barre *Cmaj7* chord. Barre at the 3rd fret above the capo, and play what looks like an *Amaj7* fingering in front of the barre (middle finger on the third string, 1st fret; ring finger on the fourth string, 2nd fret; and little finger on the second string, 2nd fret). To play the following *C#dim7* chord, simply move your middle finger from the third string to the fifth string, 1st fret. Hang onto everything else from the *Cmaj7*.

This leads to *Dm/F*, with which you are familiar from "Bookends." In the middle of measure 2, you need to arpeggiate the *Dm/F* quickly. If you can arpeggiate using your thumb and three fingers, great. If you need to strum it to imitate Simon's sound, that will work. If you strum, you will need to move your right hand back into position quickly for the descending arpeggio that finishes measure 2.

In measure 4, Simon begins a single-note accompaniment that he uses throughout the tune. The double diagonal lines in the notation signify a slight break in the flow of the rhythm. Slide from measure 4 to 5 with the middle finger on the fifth string. In measure 6, Simon picks up the tempo, using triplet eighth notes. Measure 7 contains the "Feelin' Groovy" descending passage with a twist: He starts on a *Cmaj7* and ends on a *C/G*, quickly moving to an *F* in measure 8. The *x*'s in measure 8 signify a damped strum. He strikes the strings with an upswing as he changes from an *F* to an *Eminor* chord. He then jumps right back to part of his "Feelin' Groovy" passage before moving to the *D7/F#* in measure 9. I suggest you finger the sixth string with your left thumb.

In measure 10, leave your little finger in place on the second string as you chromatically descend in the bass. The chord in measure 11 is interesting. It is three open strings with an *F* in the bass. He then bends the second string at the first fret--not such an easy task. Another damped note occurs in measure 12. Lightly touch the sixth string with your left-hand thumb as you fret the rest of the *Dm/F*. The *Dm/F* fingering then slides two frets up the neck, and you add your index finger on the first string, 3rd fret, for the *C/G** in measure 13.

There are a number of ways to finger the *G/C* in measure 13. Either barre it, with the middle finger fretting the third string in front of the barre, or think of it as a misplaced *D* fingering (3rd and 4th frets, second, third and fourth strings) with the index finger reaching out one more string to the fifth string at the 3rd fret. Barre the three treble strings for the *A* chord. Slide the barre to the first fret at the end of measure 13.

In measure 14, Simon uses a second diminished seventh fingering, this time on the four treble strings. If you aren't familiar with this fingering, try thinking of it this way: play a normal first-position *D* chord one fret higher and over one string, so that you are fretting the second, third and fourth strings. Then add your little finger on the first string, 3rd fret.

Simon's single-note idea returns in measures 16-17. Make sure you slide with the middle finger in measure 17. That will set up your fingering for the *E7* at the end of the measure. Simon introduces a *Bbmaj7* chord in measure 18. Barre this one. Measures 19-24 are repeated ideas from verse 1.

In measure 25, Garfunkel takes over the lead vocal. Simon's accompaniment is simple and tasteful, with an overdubbed 12-string becoming very apparent in this section. In measure 27, Simon's "Feelin Groovy" passage leads to a *D7/F#* in measure 28, then moves to an *F*. He repeats these two measures in 29-30. In measure 31, I have taken the liberty to include a 12-string passage on the last two beats. It is one that is very apparent, dominating the 6-string. In 32, Simon starts the "Bookends" riff, but immediately shifts to yet another diminished chord fingering, the *Dm(b5)/F*. You may want to barre this one over three strings at the first fret.

Measures 33-40 are a repeat of verse 2's accompaniment, with the exception of the *Ddim* chord at the end of measure 34. You might want to barre that chord also.

Simon's single-note passage in measure 42 ends the piece not on a *C* chord as we might expect, but rather on an *F*, the IV chord of the key of C. The feeling of uncertainty in the music nicely supports the uncertainty in the lyrics.

"Overs"

Transcribed from *Bookends*

By Paul Simon

"Overs"

"Overs"

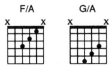

"Overs"

"Overs"

For Emily, Whenever I May Find Her

The Tune

"For Emily, Whenver I May Find Her" is another song from Simon and Garfunkel's stellar *Parsley, Sage, Rosemary and Thyme* album. This song also made it onto their *Greatest Hits* album.

Art Garfunkel's phrasing is exquisite. The notation of the vocal provides merely an adequate representation of what he actually does with the notes and words. The system of music notation that we use is simply unable to capture it all. Listen closely to the recording to feel the flow of the rhythm in his singing, and the dynamics of Simon's accompaniment.

The Technique

"For Emily, Whenever I May Find Her" is the only 12-string piece in this book. The song will sound all right played on a 6-string guitar, but won't have the brightness or the melodic interplay between the bass and treble strings. Simon regularly takes advantage of the melodic possibilities of the 12-string in this tune.

Although the tune is played with an alternating bass, the high-pitched strings of the 12-string hide that fact a bit. In the opening phrase, for instance, Simon's alternating bass on the fourth and third strings provides not only the bass notes, but also the highest pitch notes of the melody, even though he also picks the first string in the treble.

Finger a first-position *D* chord for the opening phrase, leaving the first string open. In measure 3, release the third string as well. Now you are picking only open strings.

This idea continues until measure 11, where Simon moves to a *G* chord with the first string open, a *G6*. In measure 12 he walks down in the bass to an *Eminor* chord. In measure 13 he returns to his original *Dadd9* chord, followed by a *Cmaj7, G* and *A* leading into verse 2.

Simon actually harmonizes on the first string with Garfunkel's vocal in measures 20-21. This is done simply by adding the little finger on the 3rd fret, returning to *D*, then opening the first string. Pretty simple, but effective. Measures 22-30 repeat verse 1's accompaniment.

The guitar harmony appears again in measures 31-32, but with more insistence this time, strumming the treble strings with a slight upswing between beats. This increasing dynamic leads to several full strums starting in measure 33.

In measure 43, Simon begins his guitar instrumental. You can see in measure 43 how the high-pitched third string can be used to play the melody. The melody switches back to the treble strings in measure 44.

Simon slows down the tempo a bit for emphasis in measure 49. Play those individual notes with power, as Simon does. In measure 50, he returns to his original tempo and accompaniment, this time using a *D* chord with the first and second strings open.

The power returns in measures 65 to the end, with a substantial amount of strumming. In measures 68-71, follow through with your thumb on the alternate bass note. This produces a strumming effect, since your thumb strikes more than one string. This is a very common thumb pattern among alternating-bass players in the blues idiom, and among "thumbpickers" in the Merle Travis mold.

Sustain the second-string, 3rd-fret note into the last chord. The *D/F#add4* chord is a complex sound, especially on a 12-string.

"For Emily, Whenever I May Find Her"

Transcribed from *Parsley, Sage Rosemary And Thyme*

By Paul Simon

Capo III — 12-string guitar

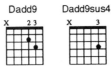

"For Emily, Whenever I May Find Her"

I wan — dered emp — ty streets down past the shop dis — plays. I heard ca — the - dral bells trip — ping down the al - ley ways

D

"For Emily, Whenever I May Find Her"

"For Emily, Whenever I May Find Her"

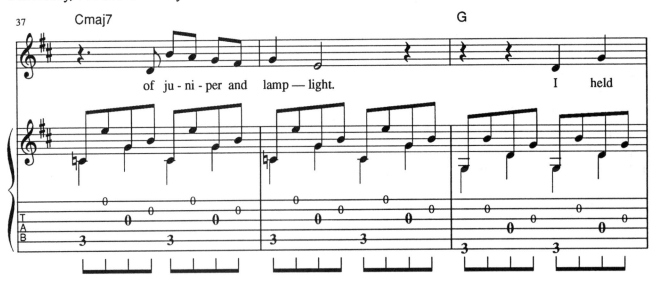

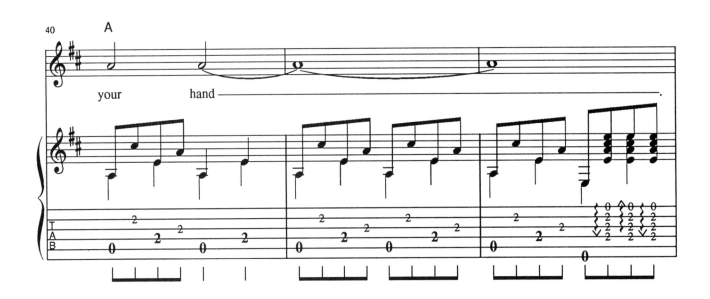

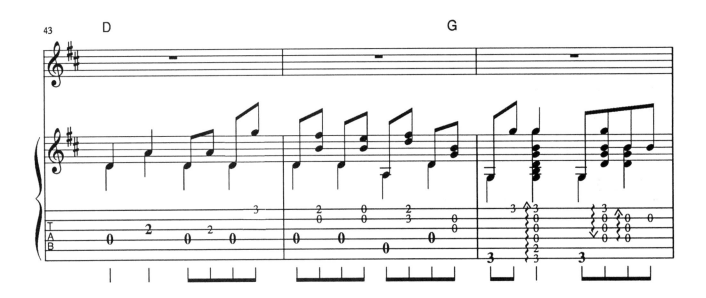

"For Emily, Whenever I May Find Her"

"For Emily, Whenever I May Find Her"

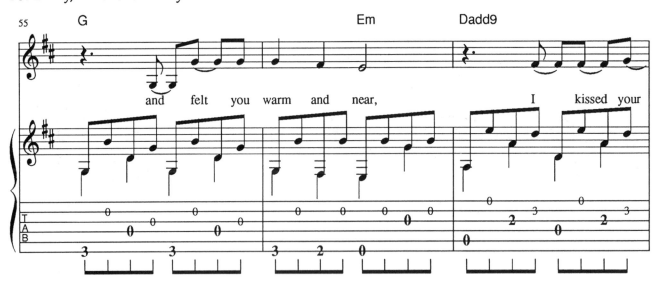

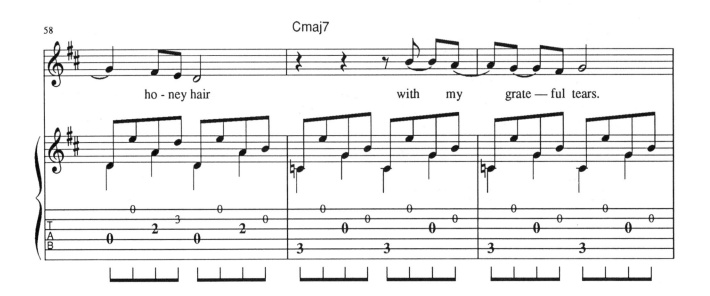

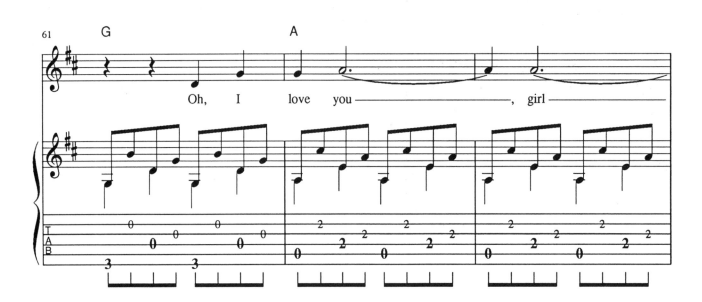

Hearts And Bones

The Tune

"Hearts And Bones" was the title track for Paul Simon's 1983 solo album. It also was included in *Negotiations And Love Songs* from 1988, and was prominently featured in *Paul Simon's Concert In Central Park* video from 1991.

The transcription of the guitar part notated here comes almost exclusively from the *Concert In Central Park* video. At certain measures where the studio version was clearer or more representative, I took the liberty to insert it. The transcription of the vocal comes from *Negotiations And Love Songs,* since there is less improvisation in the phrasing. The vocal in the Coda is from the video, however.

If you are playing along with the video you may play straight through the transcription as it is written. However, you must be aware of one idiosyncrasy: Simon deletes measure 57 from verse 1. The scanning of his lyrics required it. Simply go from measure 56 to 58 when singing verse 1. We chose to notate it as we did to save ourselves many pages of printing and save you many pages of reading. Make sure you include measure 57 in verses 2 and 3.

If you are playing along with the studio version, several changes must be made. First, the opening four measures are played *a tempo* (at normal speed), rather than rubato style (freely) as notated here. Certain measures will differ slightly-- measure 20 for instance--but not enough to make a difference. Measures 154-187 were inserted in the live version as a vehicle for a soaring Michael Brecker saxophone solo. This instrumental section should simply be omitted if you are playing along with the studio version. Skip directly from measure 153 to 188. Play 188-195 two times before returning to measure 36 for the final verse.

The Technique

Simon's main accompaniment riff can be seen in its complete form in measures 36-43. In the introduction on the video he improvises a bit, particularly with the rhythm, so you might start by learning the riff from measure 36. Then go back to the introduction to see what he does to change it.

The E* in measure 36 can be thought of as a C-type fingering (minus the ring finger on the fifth string) at the 5th and 6th frets. The right-hand picking pattern is a variation of the alternating bass, leaving out the third-beat bass note. Simon plays the second chord in measure 36 with his little finger on the second string and ring finger on the fourth. Slide those fingers to the 9th fret in measure 37 (the E**) and reach back to the 7th fret on the first string with your index finger. This two-measure phrase repeats through measure 42. In 43, simply move back to the E* for four quarter notes.

In measures 50-53, Simon plays the Travis Pick on a B chord. In 54 he plays the C#m* as an index finger barre on the fourth and fifth strings, leaving the first string open. It is a transition chord to the D#ø (half diminished) in measure 55. Pay attention to the fingering in the chord diagrams for D#ø and D#dim7. To move from one to the next you must sustain the little- and ring-finger notes, while the index and middle fingers switch strings.

In measure 59, Simon plays a three-finger C#m7 chord that moves to a three-finger F#7/C#. Maintain your little finger note on the second string, 5th fret, when changing between those two chords. In measure 63, Simon barres a Bmaj7 at the 2nd fret, and Travis picks right through measure 70 and the Amaj7 chord.

Measures 71-73 are transcribed from the studio version, mostly because the rhythm of the guitar is steady and smooth, and is easier to imitate. If you prefer to play the video version, be aware that Simon uses the same fingerings in a similar pattern. You should be able to pick it off the video knowing that.

The main riff returns with variations in measures 74-81. Barre a C#m chord at the 4th fret for measures 82-85, then back to the main riff in measure 86. He then repeats to measure 36 for verse 2.

At the end of verse 2, take the second ending at measure 94 which leads to the bridge. He continues his Travis Picking pattern on a barre A and an E until measure 107. Here he strums an E chord from the treble strings to the bass. In 117 he plays an "inside-out" Travis Pick pattern on an A chord for four measures, then strums his E again. This continues until measure 142, where he begins a slow, chromatically descending passage into the instrumental section.

I have written the instrumental section in chord-chart form, since it is not abundantly clear from the video how Simon picks the chords. A simple *p-i-m-a* or *p-i-m-p-i-m-p-i* arpeggio will work fine. The chord diagrams show the exact fingerings Simon uses during this section.

Simon's main riff returns in measure 188, leading back to the last verse (measure 36) from the *D.S.* in measure 195.

The Coda consists of Travis Picking on several chords until measure 214. Here Simon begins strumming on a first-position E chord. The interesting aspect of the strum is the accent pattern in measure 218. The accents are on the upswing strums until the downbeat of measure 215 on the repeats. Listen to the video to imitate it.

Simon plays the main riff to the end of the song.

"Hearts And Bones"

Transcribed from *Paul Simon's Concert In Central Park*

By Paul Simon

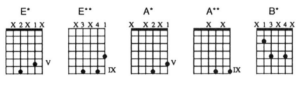

Lyrics (sung verses):

One and one-half wan- dering — Jews, free to wan —— der wher- ev- er they
back — to the sea- son be- fore. Looking back through the cracks in the
One and one-half wan- dering — Jews, re- turned to their na- tu- ral

choose ——, are trav' — ling to- ge- ther in the San- gre de Cris- to, the
door ——. Two peo- ple were mar- ried —; the act — was out- ra- geous; the
coasts ——. To re- sume — old ac- quain- tan- ces; step out occa — sionally,

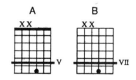

A   B

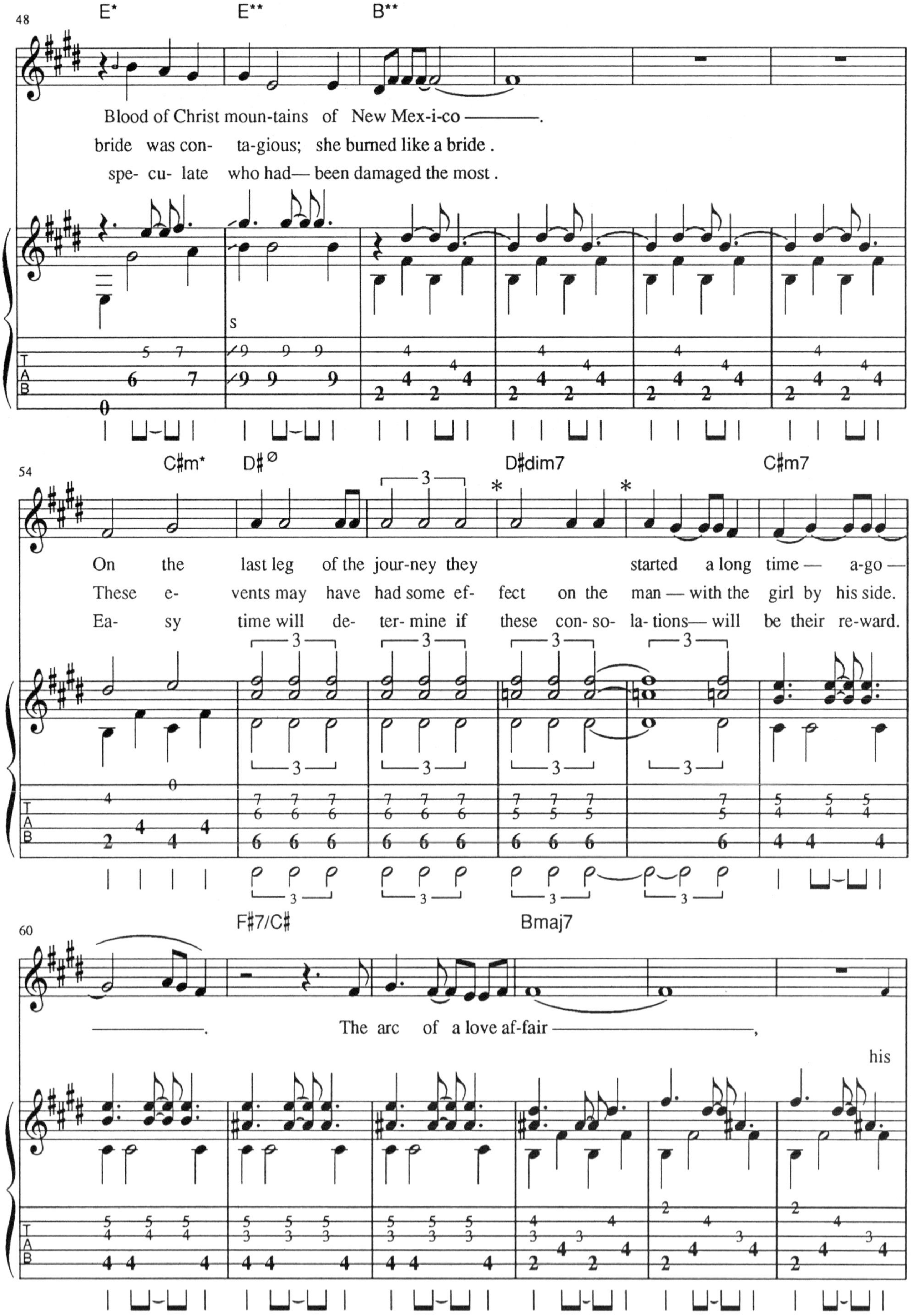

48
E* E** B**
Blood of Christ moun-tains of New Mex-i-co ———.
bride was con- ta-gious; she burned like a bride .
spe- cu- late who had— been damaged the most .
54
C♯m* D♯ø D♯dim7 C♯m7
On the last leg of the jour-ney they started a long time — a-go —
These e- vents may have had some ef- fect on the man — with the girl by his side.
Ea- sy time will de- ter- mine if these con- so- la- tions— will be their re-ward.
60
F♯7/C♯ Bmaj7
———. The arc of a love af-fair ———,
his

B**
X 1 3 3 3 X
C♯m*
X 1 1 X X
D♯ø
X 1 3 2 4 X
VI
D♯dim7
X 2 3 1 4 X
V
C♯m7
X 1 X 2 4 X
IV
F♯7/C♯
X 2 X 1 4 X
Bmaj7

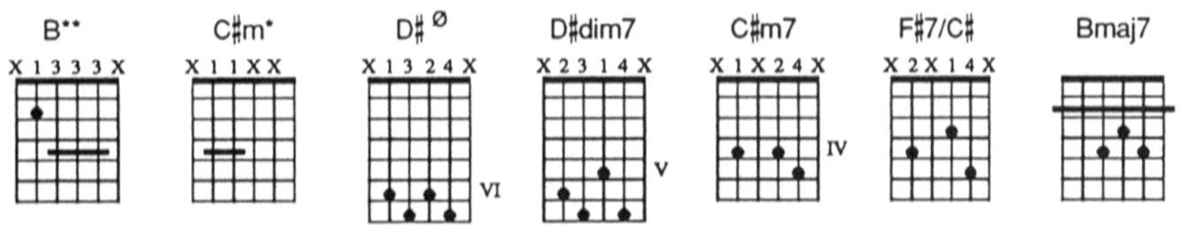

"Hearts And Bones"

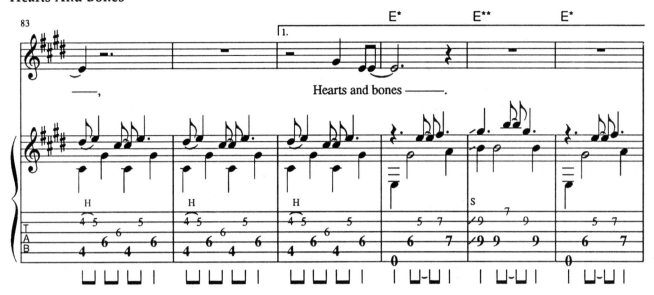

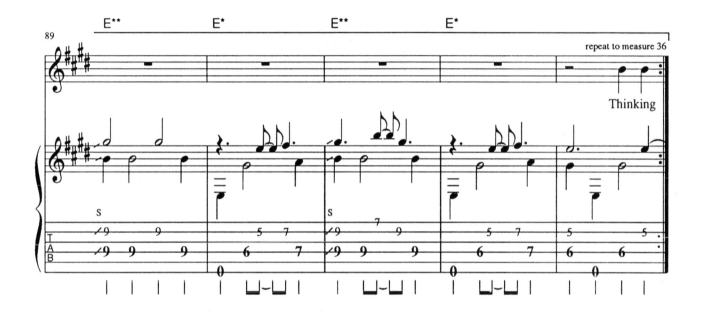

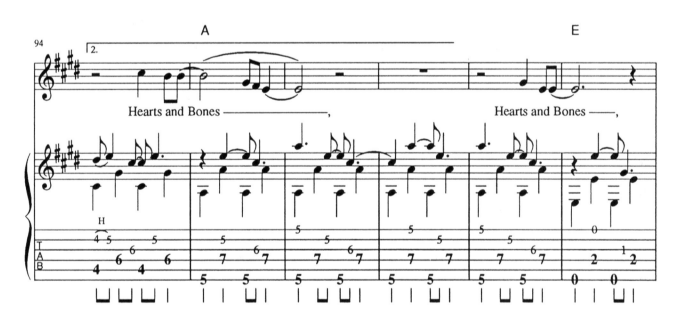

"Hearts And Bones"

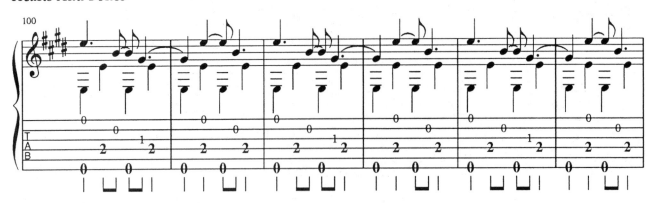

Whoa ——————, she said, Why ——————————————,

A

why don't we drive through the night? We'll wake up down in —— Mex- i- co ——————.

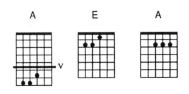

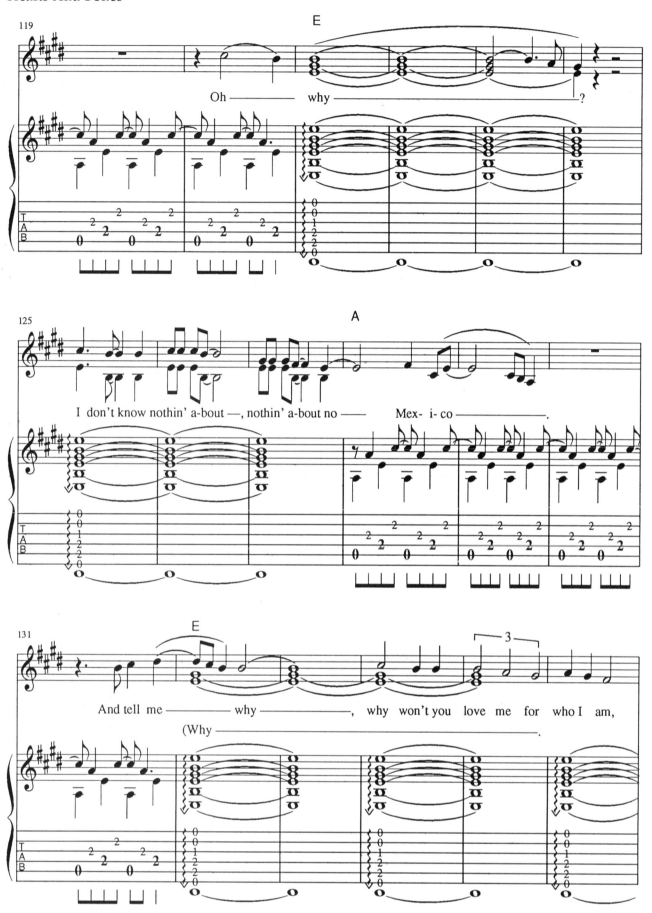

"Hearts And Bones"

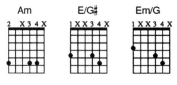

"Hearts And Bones"

Saxophone Instrumental
(from live version)

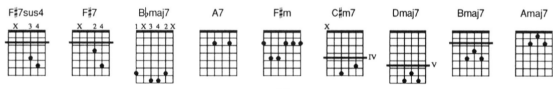

"Hearts And Bones"

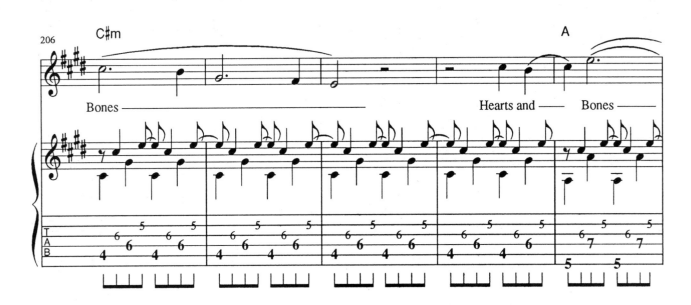

90

"Hearts And Bones"

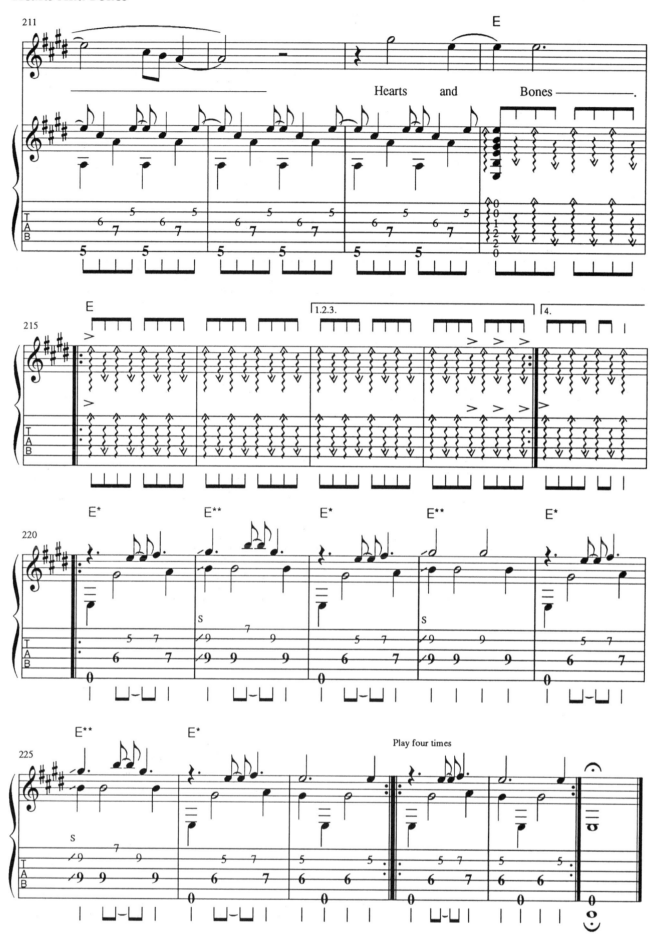

Hearts   and   Bones

Play four times

91

Tablature Guide

Tablature (TAB) is a music notation system designed to show guitarists at which fret to depress a string when picking it. It has been in existence for centuries: Lutenists in the time of the European Renaissance used a distinctive form of tablature.

Tablature has two main advantages over standard notation: 1) it clearly indicates the position on the guitar neck of each note; and 2) it is much easier to learn to read. If you don't currently read either standard notation or tablature, I recommend that you learn to read tablature. You'll be playing the pieces in this book much sooner than if you take the time to learn standard notation.

Six horizontal lines represent the six strings of the guitar:

Ex. 1)

Notice in tablature that the bass string of the guitar is represented by the *bottom* line of the staff. The treble string is the *top* line. This is inverted from the way the strings actually lie on the guitar. The reason for the inversion is simply to make tablature look more like standard notation: the low-pitched notes are on the bottom lines of the staff, and the high-pitched notes are on the top lines.

A number on a line indicates at which fret to depress that string as you pick it. **Bold-type** numbers designate notes picked by the thumb. Lighter-type numbers are notes picked by the fingers, or are slurred notes (hammer-ons, pull-offs or slides):

Ex. 2)

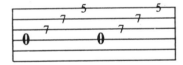

In Example 2 you pick the strings in this order:

1) fourth string open ("0" means an open string);
2) the third string fretted at the 7th fret;
3) the second string fretted at the 7th fret;
4) the first (treble) string fretted at the 5th fret;
5) then repeat the four notes.

The stems and beams underneath the notes denote the rhythm:

Ex. 3)

In Example 3, there are eight eighth-notes, each receiving one-half beat in 4/4 time. To produce the correct rhythm in Example 3, count evenly "1 & 2 & 3 & 4 &" along with the notes as you pick them.

Other rhythmic markings that you will see below the staff are (in 4/4 time):

| = quarter note (1 beat)   ♪ '= eighth note (1/2 beat)

|˙ = dotted quarter (1-1/2 beats)   ▬ = two sixteenth notes (1/2 beat)

♩ = half note (2 beats)   ▬▬ = four sixteenth notes (1 beat)

o = whole note (4 beats)   𝄽 = quarter-note rest (rest for 1 beat)

There are several other markings in tablature that you will need to know as well.

⟐ = harmonic at the 12th fret   —x— = left- or right-hand damp (mute)

v · · · · = barre at the 5th fret   1/2 VII = barre over three strings, 7th fret

|⌒| = tie (sustain the note for the duration
     of the "tied" rhythmic markings)

"H" designates a hammer-on--sounding a note by fretting a string sharply with a finger of the left hand. "P" stands for pull-off--sounding a note by plucking a string with a finger of the left hand. "B" stands for bend--stretching the string to the side as the note is ringing.

"S" stands for slide--sounding a note by sliding to it from another fret position on that string. An ascending diagonal line (/) means to slide from a lower pitch to a higher pitch. A descending diagonal line means the opposite.

If a diagonal line directly connects two numbers, you sound the first note distinctly before sliding to the second. If a number is preceded by a diagonal line that is *not* connected to another number, then the left-hand finger must already be sliding on the string when you pick it. This technique provides the sound of the slide, but no distinct pitch before the notated number.

A dot placed over a note or a chord designates "staccato." That means to release the note or chord immediately after it is picked. Most often this technique is accomplished by relaxing the fingers of the left hand, but not removing them from the strings. The fingers mute the strings, preventing what might otherwise sound like a pull-off.

A curly line next to a chord in the tablature means to strum the chord, or to arpeggiate the chord quickly with the fingers or thumb and fingers of the right hand.

For all of its attributes, tablature certainly has its disadvantages as well. The biggest deficiency of tablature is that it does not indicate how long to sustain each note. There are methods of indicating sustain in tablature, but they are difficult to read. The best solution to this problem is your sense of hearing. Listen closely to the original recordings to determine the duration of the notes.

Other Books From Mark Hanson and Accent On Music

The Art Of Contemporary Travis Picking
Recommended by *Acoustic Guitar Magazine*

A comprehensive study of the patterns and variations of the modern alternating-bass fingerpicking guitar style. This book and 90-minute cassette take you from the basic patterns up through your first two solo pieces. All exercises and tunes are played at half- and full-speed on the tape. Great for beginning fingerpickers and for more advanced players who want to understand this style. 14 tunes.

The Art Of Solo Fingerpicking
Recommended by Leo Kottke and John Renbourn

This book and 90-minute cassette thoroughly describe the intermediate-to-advanced picking techniques associated with some of today's greatest fingerpicking masters. There are 13 solo instrumentals, plus "White House Blues" from John Renbourn. All exercises and tunes are played at half- and full-speed on the tape. You'll add some hot techniques to your repertoire with this package. *Formerly Solo Style.*

The Complete Book of Alternate Tunings

By far the most comprehensive publication on alternate guitar tunings available. This book lists and explains hundreds of tunings used by such diverse artists as Michael Hedges, Chet Atkins, the Rolling Stones, and Nirvana. Includes comprehensive listing of tunings by artist. More than likely, everthing you ever wanted to know about alternate tunings, and more, is in this book.

Fingerstyle Noël

Includes a full-length listening CD! This is our highly successful Christmas book/CD package. The 80-page book includes 30 Christmas tunes, arranged for solo fingerstyle guitar, ranging in difficulty from easy to advanced. Sing-along lyrics, chords, and capo positions also included. "It's hard to imagine a more complete Christmas-guitar package." --*Guitar Player Magazine*. Standard notation and tablature.

The Music Of Leo Kottke

This book and 90-minute teaching cassette present some of Kottke's best fingerstyle guitar work in an easy-to-understand format. The note-for-note transcriptions are from Kottke's actual recordings. Mark's cassette features each entire tune played at half-speed, plus measure-by-measure instruction. TAB/standard notation. "Busted Bicycle," "Jesu, Joy," "Theme From 'The Rick & Bob Report'" and more.

Leo Kottke Transcribed

More high-quality Leo Kottke transcriptions, accompanied by Mark's measure-by-measure teaching cassette. Tunes include "William Powell," "Times Twelve," "A Trout Toward Noon," and more. Standard notation/TAB. Same format as *The Music Of Leo Kottke*.

Beginning Slide Guitar

This book tells you all you need to know about slide technique: how to set up your guitar, types of slides and hand positions, damping, fretboard "visualization," playing slide in standard and open tunings, and much more. Includes appendixes on making your own bottleneck, recommended listening , and sources for slide guitar music. *Audio Teaching Cassette available through Accent On Music*

Acoustic Jam Trax Series

Jam along with Mark and his band, the B-Street Irregulars, in this series of tapes covering a wide range of acoustic styles. Styles include acoustic blues, acoustic rock, swing, country, bluegrass, folk, and more. The accompanying books thoroughly describe how to solo over the band for each tune. Titles: *Acoustic Jam Trax, Acoustic Blues,* and *Acoustic Rock.* Standard notation and tablature.

And many more!

Distributed by Music Sales Corporation, New York, NY
For more information, inquire at your local music dealer or contact Accent On Music

Shipping & Handling Chart
Most orders are shipped within 24 hours of receipt.

	USA*	Canada/Mexico**	Europe (Airmail)	Far East/Africa (Airmail)
$24.00 and under, add	$3.95	$4.50	$10.00	$10.50
$24.01 to $50.00, add	$4.95	$5.50	$12.00	$14.00
$50.01 to $75.00, add	$5.95	$6.50	$17.00	$21.00
$75.01 to $100.00, add	$6.95	$7.50	$22.00	$28.00
$100.01 to $140.00, add	$7.95	$8.50	$28.00	$36.00
$140.01 to $200.00, add	$8.95	$9.50	$35.00	$48.00
$200.00 and over, please call				

*For USA: add $2.00 for Priority Mail. **For Canada/Mexico: add $2.50 for Priority Mail.

Order Form

	Catalog Number	Price
• RECENT RELEASES		
The Complete Book of Alternate Tunings	AM 7044	$16.95
Fingerstyle Noël (book & CD)	6044BK	$19.95
Yuletide Guitar (CD)	6044CD	$12.95
Yuletide Guitar (Cassette)	6044CS	$ 9.95
• ACOUSTIC MUSICIAN™ TAPE+TAB SERIES		
The Music of Leo Kottke (book & cassette)	T 301	$19.95
Leo Kottke Transcribed (book & cassette)	T 302	$19.95
Mark Hanson: Standard & Drop-D Tunings (book & cassette)	T 201	$17.95
• INSTRUCTION BOOKS		
Paul Simon Transcribed (book)	AM 4044	$19.95
The Acoustic Guitar of Martin Simpson (book)	AM 5044	$17.95
Art of Contemporary Travis Picking (book & cassette)	AM 1044	$18.95
Art of Solo Fingerpicking (formerly *Solo Style*; book & cassette)	AM 2044	$19.95
• "GUITAR CASE" SERIES		
Beginning Slide Guitar (book & cassette)	MS 020	$12.95
12-String Guitar Guide (book)	MS 030	$ 5.95
Acoustic Jam Trax (All styles: Blues, Folk, Country, Rock, Funk; book & cassette)	MS 040	$12.95
Acoustic Rock Jam Trax (Acoustic Rock; book & cassette)	MS 050	$12.95
Acoustic Blues Jam Trax (Acoustic Blues; book & cassette)	MS 060	$12.95

• COMPACT DISCS • CASSETTES • VIDEOS
We carry a variety of recordings and videos. Please write for a complete listing

Catalog No.	Product	Quantity	x	Unit Price	=	Amount

SUBTOTAL $_____

SHIPPING AND HANDLING: (See chart on adjoining page) $_____

California State Sales Tax (7.25%--based on Subtotal from above). California residents only. $_____

Add $2.00 for domestic Priority Mail (1st Class). $_____

TOTAL: $_____

TO ORDER:

Call (503) 699-1814, FAX (503) 699-1813, E-Mail: accentm@teleport.com

or send VISA/MASTERCARD/MONEY ORDER/CHECK (US$ drawn on a US bank), payable to:

Accent On Music, Dept. 4044, 19363 Willamette Dr. #252, West Linn, OR 97068 USA.

Refund (excluding S/H) within 30 days only. Returned items must be in original condition. Opened CDs and tapes are non-returnable.

Name_____

Address_____

City_____State_____ZIP_____

Country_____Telephone: Day (_____)_____Eve (_____)_____

VISA/MC No.   ___ ___ ___ ___ - ___ ___ ___ ___ - ___ ___ ___ ___ - ___ ___ ___ ___   Exp. Date___ ___-___ ___

Signature_____

Paul Simon Discography

Simon & Garfunkel

Album	Release Date	Label/Catalog No.
Wednesday Morning, 3AM	1964	Columbia-9049
Sounds of Silence	1965	Columbia-9269
Parsley, Sage, Rosemary and Thyme	1967	Columbia-9363
The Graduate	1967	Columbia-3180
Bookends	1968	Columbia-9529
Bridge Over Troubled Water	1970	Columbia-9914
Simon & Garfunkel's Greatest Hits	1972	Columbia-31950
With Art Garfunkel-*Breakaway*	1975	Columbia-33700
With Art Garfunkel & James Taylor-*Watermark*	1978	Columbia-34975
Collected Works	1981	Columbia-45322
The Concert In Central Park	1982	Warner Bros.-3654
The Concert In Central Park (Video)	1982	CBS-Fox Video--CV600133

Paul Simon Solo

Album	Release Date	Label/Catalog No.
Paul Simon	1972	Warner Bros.-25588
There Goes Rhymin' Simon	1973	Warner Bros.-25589
Live Rhymin'	1974	Warner Bros.-25590
Still Crazy After All These Years	1975	Warner Bros.-25591
Paul Simon-Greatest Hits, Etc.	1977	Columbia-35032
One-Trick Pony	1980	Warner Bros.-HS3472
Paul Simon In Concert (Video)	1980	Warner Home Video-34005
Hearts and Bones	1983	Warner Bros.-23942
Graceland	1986	Warner Bros.-25447
Graceland (Video)	1987	Warner Reprise-38136-3
Negotiations and Love Songs	1988	Warner Bros.-25789
Rhythm of the Saints	1990	Warner Bros.-26098
Paul Simon's Concert In The Park	1991	Warner Bros.-26737
Paul Simon's Concert In The Park (Video)	1991	Warner Reprise-38277-3

Acknowledgments

A sincere thank you goes to the people at Paul Simon Music for their kind assistance in this project. Special thanks to Ian Hoblyn, Eleanor Swan, and Mark Silag for their help in making this book a reality.

I can't thank the folks at Music Sales Corporation enough. Barrie Edwards, Dan Early, and particularly Dave McCumiskey have been instrumental in the production and distribution of this book.

Others who helped immensely include these fine people: Henry Grossman for the cover photograph; Chris Ledgerwood for the masterful cover design; Mac computer guru and Simon aficionado Patrick Mahoney; *DRUM! Magazine* founder Phil Hood for his endless support and encouragement; the crew at Gryphon Stringed Instruments in Palo Alto, California; Pearwood Graphics; and the innumerable guitar students I have had over the past two decades who have taught me how to teach. Also, my family deserves the highest praise for allowing me the time to produce such an immense project.

The biggest thank you of course goes to Paul Simon himself. Without his artistry and inspiration, none of this would be possible.

About The Author

Mark Hanson worked as an Associate Editor and columnist at *Frets Magazine* until its demise in 1989. He is a performing guitarist as well as a writer, guitar instructor and publisher. He owns and operates Accent On Music, which publishes *The Music Of Leo Kottke* book-plus-teaching-tape package, the *Acoustic Musician™ Tape+TAB Series* of taped guitar lessons, as well as Mark's teaching methods on the alterating-bass style of fingerpicking guitar.

His interview subjects include such luminaries as James Taylor, David Crosby, Jorma Kaukonen, Larry Carlton, Michael Hedges, John Renbourn and Alex deGrassi. Mark's accurate and thorough guitar transcriptions have appeared regularly in both *Guitar Player* and *Frets*. Mark's background includes a music degreee from Stanford University, and over twenty years of teaching and performing experience.